HOW DARE YOU!
360 DEGREES-DUKEISM

By: Melvin L. Dukes, Jr.

McClure Publishing, Inc.
Bloomingdale, IL 60108

Copyright © 2013

All rights reserved. Printed and bound in the United States of America. According to the 1976 United States Copyright Act, no part of this book may be reproduced or utilized in any form or by any means, electronic or mechanical, including photocopying, recording, or by any information storage or retrieval system, except by a reviewer who may quote brief passages in a review to be printed in a magazine or newspaper, without permission in writing from the Publisher: Inquiries should be addressed to McClure Publishing, Inc. Permissions Department, 358 West Army Trail Road, #205, Bloomingdale, Illinois 60108.

The author and publisher have made every effort to ensure the accuracy and completeness of information contained in this book, we assume no responsibility for errors, inaccuracies, omissions, or any inconsistency therein.

2nd Edition – July 15, 2013
LCCN: 2013949966
ISBN 13: 978-0-9833697-5-2

LCCN: TXu 807-476 – May 19, 1997 1st Edition

Cover Design and Interior Layout by Kathy McClure
Cover Design Idea - Author Melvin L. Dukes, Jr.

http://mcclurepublishing.wix.com/books

To order additional copies, please contact
Melvin L. Dukes, Jr.
at melvindjr@yahoo.com.

I dedicate this book
to those who understand DUKEISM.
Everyone has their own philosophy about life.

INTRODUCTION

Allow me to introduce myself, my name is Ricky. This is a true story about life (*the names have been changed to protect the innocent*). I hope that you will find something in this book that may pertain to what you have experienced and that it will help you succeed in life.

How Dare You – 360 Degrees-Dukeism has been at the Library of Congress since 1997 it is as new now as it was then. This is the 2nd Edition.

This story depicts the life and experiences of what I had to go through from a child to my adult life. The awfulness of not having food, clean clothes and a decent place to stay, caused me to focus more on developing survival skills than on my education which almost left me illiterate.

The street life I saw everyday was a hard knocks life which seems as if every sphere was working against me. I grew up with hustlers, pimps, prostitutes, and drug attics who taught me that I should watch my back in a cruel society that is filled with destruction.

I was born in Cleveland, Ohio, to Georgia Joann Davis. We called her Ma-Dear. Her maiden name was Smith. I have a vague memory of my Father from birth until I was one and half years old. The only recollection I have of that time span is throwing my bottle out of the window and Ma-Dear searching around for it.

When I turned one and a half, I recall a man coming on the scene stating that he was not my Father. From there the wheels of life started turning in so many different direction.

CHAPTER ONE

A smoked filled night club with people sitting two to four per table, lining the bar stools against the bar waiting on the performance of Ricky Davis, Sr.

The club announcer grabs the MIC and says, "We are bringing to the stage the one and only Ricky Davis."

Applauds echoing and piercing off the walls of the room while Ricky walks on to the stage, puts one hand on the MIC and says in a deep bass voice, "Ladies," women screaming while the words of, "We LOVE you Ricky!" fills the room.

He began each performance making sure his clothes matched and dressed to *kill*.

After the performance, he rushes back to his dressing room to get just one more hit. He pulls the drugs out of his bag, sets everything on the table near the couch, and starts cooking. When he knew it was ready, he took a cotton ball and the syringe and pulled the heroin in through the needle. After wrapping the rubber holes around his arm, he hit his arm so that the vein would be ready and then he filled his vein with the poison in the needle.

Ricky thought it was the only way to survive. Once he got the first hit, it was over for us. This was a life we had to live with until we were able to stand on our own. Nodding off for about 20 minutes, he gets up from the couch and gets a snicker's candy bar out of the candy bowl that sits on the table lighting a cigarette all at the same time.

The man I called my Father was very talented. His audience loves his performance because every time he performed he added something fresh and new.

It was time for his last performance that night so he got up from the couch to get himself together. Running back to the stage for the grand finale, Ricky left his audience begging for more.

He leaves the club, jumps in his car and drives right off the side of the road. When the police notice a car in the ditch, they decide to pull over to check it out.

One officer walks over to the car holding his flash light shining it against the driver's side window. Knocking on the glass the officer says, "Are you alright, sir?" No response. "Are you alright, sir?" Ricky looks up and rolls down the window with his head down saying, "Yes officer. I'm fine."

"Registration and license please…."

He reached in the glove compartment only to find that he didn't have current papers on the car. Hesitant to tell the police officer, he sat up in the car thinking how he could explain without being arrested.

The officer says, "Get out of the car. Put your hands on the hood." He walked dad to the hood of the car and started searching him.

Since dad was dragging his feet and did not respond fast enough the officers ran his license plates and found that they had been suspended, so they took him down to the slammer.

Oh boy. How is dad going to get his drugs? Finger prints came back with warrants from a crime he committed and did not come to court on his scheduled court date.

* * *

One morning, I was sitting on the floor, playing with a fire truck and this man came in and told me to go home. I didn't understand what he was talking about—he had on a pair of boxers on and was walking around, but he told me to go home. I kept playing with my truck because I didn't understand what he was saying. I really didn't pay much attention to him….

At that time, I was the third child (*there were two children before me—Ronald, who was born in 1955 and Regina, born in 1956*). I was doing pretty well up until this point.

I was born in Cleveland, Ohio at Mount Sinai Hospital. The area around the hospital looked like skid row. Homeless people living on the street, trash was everywhere. It was dark and gloomy.

My Mother (Ma-Dear), from what I can remember and know, was real busy working the streets turning tricks to help make ends meet. By this time she had six kids. She got really sick by the age of 28 and passed away soon thereafter.

Ma-Dear was trying to keep up with my Father who wanted to be an entertainer. He had just been released from jail (*earlier*) when he told me to go home. He used to make it very clear to me that he wasn't my Father. He was a smooth guy, a slick hustler.

Ma-Dear would do anything this man (my Father) would tell her to do, just to get his attention and to be loved by him. This man used to constantly beat her, then he'd disappear for years, and when he returned, he would send her through more changes—mess up the relationships she may have had with her other male friends, which would account for some of the things she had to do to feed us, because we were on Public Aid (ADC).

Remember back in the 60s when the Department of Public Aid, would send a caseworker out to your house; you weren't allowed to have a man in your house. They would come in, search the house and see if they could find any men's clothing laying about—we had to hide the telephones, TVs, some extra lamps and other stuff, so they wouldn't see it; because by people being poor and on ADC, they weren't allowed to have such items. Ma-Dear, would do the best she could with what she had, even sell her body in order to make ends meet.

We were always surrounded by clever people, gays, lesbians, hustlers, and *slicksters*, you name it; bums, older people that were supposed to have been well-to-do, at the same time they were trying to get whatever sexual favors they could out of Ma-Dear, this included relatives, they had their share of using her.

She drank Richard's Wild Irish Rose heavily, so I guess she drank herself to death. She would go on the *stroll* and sometimes her relatives would come by and *snatch us up* because she would be gone for weeks at a time, all the while, they were treating us really badly; good thing we were able to fend for ourselves.

My sister Regina, being a year older than me knew how to do a little bit of this and a little bit of that. Being the oldest girl, she could write a little bit and was the speller of the family. She would always help us spell little things.

We knew how to keep the house clean, how to be invisible around grown-ups and take care of each other, even though we were surrounded by, from my point of view gorgeous ladies, handsome gentlemen and well-to-do people, but this was not your typical environment.

I attended a public school called, Wave Park, (*the first school I ever attended*) then we went to John D. Rockefeller, then we transferred back to Wave Park. Most of the buildings are torn down now. We were able to walk from Nicholas, which was close to Wave Park, way over to around East 76th Street in Cleveland, Ohio, where my Grandmother used to live. She was a very clever woman, she did her thing, but she always knew how to survive and she had a lot of common sense.

Whenever my Father would pop in from out of town or wherever, he would have sex with my Mother and then beat her and destroy the house and whatever little bit of furniture we had. He just upset everything.

After witnessing all this abuse; all that drama really made us stronger. My siblings and I really didn't have a certain time that we had to come in, so we did what we could which was called "***hustle*** pop bottles" when we lived on Nicholas, pushing the bottles around in a buggy, washing them until they were clean, and then taking them over to the grocery store for five cents per bottle.

We would buy food, a little candy and stuff. At neighborhood parties, people would throw away all of their pop bottles, (*pops came in bottles at that particular time*). So that the sweet syrup in the bottles would not attract roaches, we would take the pop bottles and wash them out and turn them in the next day. We had a system going. Then we would eat our candy or food, and things of this nature.

Once, I remember when we were small—Easter came around; we didn't celebrate holidays, but this particular Easter we were sharp; me, Ronald, David and Regina; I'm not sure if Wendy was—I'm quite sure Wendy wasn't on the set at that particular time, or JuJu, (*my younger sister and brother*) but we were sharp!

We had on a hat and a shark-skinned suit, this suit was shiny, bluish-grayish, reddish looking color. We would wear the hat that Grandmother gave us, we were sharp! I can remember that Easter clear as day.

The way they measured our heads for the hats—they would take a piece of newspaper, roll it up and put it around the sides of our heads and cuff 'em in, that's how they got the hats to fit our heads, and we were sharp! The shoes, the works, even new underwear. That's one of the first times I can remember getting decent underwear.

My Mother was young when she started having kids. She had to have been a teenager, somewhere, when she started having us. I just know she was very young. She went out one time and didn't come back; I mean, this had to be like almost two weeks, and we were still functioning.

Then one day, again, my Mother's relatives came over and got us; they didn't say anything, they just started grabbing us and Ma-Dear already told us, don't let anybody in and don't go with anybody because she would be very upset when she got back and we were gone, so we would do as we were told because this was the environment we lived in. Like I said, we were able to function and fend for ourselves even while Ma-Dear wasn't there.

The relatives came in and took all of us out of there, I was hiding under the bed, trying not to go, and they were telling us that my Mother was in the hospital. Even after going with our relatives for a while, we somehow got back home, but mom was still gone.

One day I was in the playground, swinging on a swing, I knew what they wanted. I thought to myself *why were they looking for me? I kind of felt she had passed*, so my Father had to get all the kids together and try to buy us clothes.

Our Father had come up from Detroit with one of his girlfriend's name Mama Christy. Mama Christy looked like a nurse to us, she was a little lady but she was smart as a whip; she already had three kids; now with three kids and six kids, that gave you nine, with two adults, that gave you eleven mouths to feed.

*   *   *

Now way before this had happened, let's say the early 60s again, my Father got shot in the backyard on 77th Street. He was singing with some friends and they got into an argument, I think he was trying to save somebody, but he got shot and he almost died, *I'm quite sure he was probably on Heroin*, but when he came home from the hospital, he really was on Heroin because of the morphine he had to take for pain while recovering. Morphine is very addictive. When he couldn't get the morphine, Heroin was the next best drug. He had his little Cocaine and things and then he disappeared again.

We had an Aunt name Wendy that used to look out for us, and she helped my Mother and my Grand mama take care of us while they were going back and forth to the hospital, so eventually our Father got out, he still wanted to be a singer and they had different groups performing in different places. He would tell jokes that were so funny that he was able to be on the Jean Carol Show in Cleveland.

Like I said, he would disappear, and we didn't see him that often and then we ended up the way we were in the 60s. When they came in and got us, after Ma-Dear passed—it was a quick funeral and then we were wondering if we were going to Detroit Michigan; because we hadn't seen our Father that often, we really didn't know what was going to happen to us.

While we were driving to Detroit, he asked us, "What do you want to do?" My other brothers and sisters, (*a few of them*) didn't know what to do. Me being the Ricky that I am told them, let's take a vote, so we took a vote; although it wasn't like we sat down and had a board meeting about it--I simply asked everybody who wanted to go with Grandma Smith, raise their hands? I raised my hand, didn't nobody else raise theirs. Then I asked them, who all want to go with our Father, raise your hand? All of them raised their hands. The decision was unanimous. Most of them chose to stay with our Father.

When we got to where we were going, Mama Christy was making us clean up and treating us like slaves, but we would already do what we had to do. She was more or less a little more organized than what we were accustomed to, but we were not really paying attention because we really missed Ma-Dear. This was right after Ma-Dear had passed. I took it really hard.

On my Father's side, the relatives pitched in to make us look fairly decent for the funeral. As I mentioned, we had to take a vote on where we wanted to go—did we want to go with the Smith's—that treated us bad? Or, did we want to go with this father, whom we really didn't know.

We saw how badly he treated our Mother, through the years, off and on; the man whom they call my Father. Although he made it perfectly clear to me that he wasn't my Father, even though I have his name, Ricky Leroy Davis Jr. Leroy was one of his brothers' names this is how I got my middle name.

We stayed there for a good two or three weeks watching what was going on, so when we--I think Grandma Smith was trying to get us, our Father took us because he was the father, and his name was Davis, all of us had the same last name, Davis, except my oldest brother Ronald, whose last name was the same as my Mother's maiden name, Smith.

Most of us look different; we don't have the same resemblances like brothers and sisters. My Father, Ricky Davis, Sr. would state that Regina, David and JuJu were his children. Ronald, Wendy and me weren't. Wendy got to meet her father before he died. Ronald never met his father.

The person they told me was my Father (*Sam Jones*) wouldn't even acknowledge me as his son. Ricky Sr. took me to his house one time, after that I never went back again.

Sam had a wife and another son who looked just like me. The one time I visited, we played with toys, with a train set, and went swimming, but as I said, this gentleman didn't claim or acknowledge me as his son and he never denied it either. Because of that, I call this man who I am named after Ricky Davis, Sr., my Father.

While we were growing up, our Father was so smooth and so clever. The drugs that are out now, it's nothing like Heroin. Heroin was a thinking man's dope. Heroin, after you shoot it, made you feel better. If you didn't have it, you got really sick, it would tear you up; just tear out your guts; make you want to throw up because you had to have it or you couldn't function--you couldn't even use the washroom unless you had your fix of Heroin.

Once you get the Heroin in your system, you turn into Einstein. It put you in a state of a *nod*. When we call it a nod, that means you're just there, you're awake, you can hear what's going on around you, but you're so relaxed that you don't want to move--you're just in a nod. It's a drug that makes you sleep walk even though you are really awake.

The only reason I can explain this feeling so deep, is because I tried to feel it. See, I never shot dope or anything, but I would try to be that person; try to imagine the mood it had them in. They have this thing on their face called a *mask*. A mask is the way you look when the dope is in you, it's a hard look. It is a look that's…. You know, you just get out of that person's way when you see them with that mask on.

The manufacturers of the dope on the street, came up with this new dope, *(new to us that is. I'm sure it's been around for a long time...)* Blows (*Heroin*) and Rocks (Cocaine). Blows and Rocks make you do things unconsciously; you just do stuff, you don't even think about it.

CHAPTER TWO

After we moved to Detroit, our Father, was still trying to be a singer, he had a group called Scorpio and Libra. They were doing local gigs; they had a record out called "I *Ain't* Playing Baby" and "Going Out The World Backwards." They were supposed to have gotten contracts to do something else because a lot of people thought dad was very talented; he was a slick guy, he would run different con games and stunts in order to survive. Our Father would do anything he could to get his drugs.

At this point, things were falling apart with the singing, my Mother had died, he had six kids and he was with a woman that had three. As I said before, Mama Christy was very bright. This woman could read, write, do shorthand, and get a job anywhere she wanted but she loved our Father so much that she wanted to be with him all the time. The environment was so slick and so clever that she wanted just to be there. She took care of us--she would write checks--some of them would bounce and they would do everything in their power not to get caught and told us to say they're not home.

We were getting older and getting ready to transfer to another school--they put us back because when you go from city to city, you are held back a year. We did not know the fundamentals of the three R's: reading, writing, and arithmetic; we were introduced to it but we knew more of the street life.

In Cleveland, we went from place to place. We never really got established in order to learn the norms of reading, writing and arithmetic. We moved to Detroit in an area called Roselawn. Today, it's an expressway--they bought the school. The highway ran straight through our neighborhood, which my Father was not trying to move out. The place was already condemned. We still had electricity and gas, but he waited until the eleventh hour.

We got put out by the side of the expressway. It was so many of us. When we ate, we never got full and it wasn't like we got a chance to sit down and have breakfast before we went to school--with nine kids? We had to eat whatever we could find.

The six of us knew how to take care of one another. Because of the Heroin habit dad had, we never did see Christmas and celebrate holidays, but we had fun. We got things like Jacks, bat & ball, marbles, hula-hoops, and toys called footsies. By it being six of us, we were always entertaining ourselves--we never had TVs or radios or things like this, but when we did, it would be something that would be on the brink of breaking or going out otherwise dad would try and sell it.

Mama Christy's children Frank, Kim and Steve who were younger than us got treated better because their father would come and assist with taking care of them. He would buy their clothes and take them places without us so that he could bond with his children. It was still hard for them also because they lived with us.

My brother Ronald, had no education but as far as electronics, (*back to when we were younger*) he could work miracles with a battery, a piece of string and some wire or whatever he could get his hands on--old TV's, and make them work. It may not have had any sound to it, but we had a TV and we always had a little piece of radio around the house, they'd be so raggedy. This was done before the old man even got on the set. We would break something and Ronald would fix it. They used to tell us how slow he was, but he was fast enough to understand the way of life and how things functioned.

We might have been slow as far as books were concern which was the furthest thing from our minds. The most important thing on our mind was feeding each other and taking care of one another. When we went to school, we would get up early enough to arrive at school and these kids would bring their lunches. The other children would set their lunches on the side so that we could play before school started. Now have you, we would be hungry in the morning.

Before we went to class, everybody would be playing in the playground, they played games called "*It*" or jumping rope--we would get one brother or sister to get up and start the game called "*It*". Five of us would call what we were going to get out of the other children's lunch bags. We had a plan.

This is what we would do: some of us would sit next to somebody's lunch while the other one would be playing "*It*" or whatever. The ones sitting next to the lunches would get about three lunches. Then we would start claiming how we would divvy it up. One of us would say, "I got the apple," the other would say, "I got the banana, I got the sandwich, I got this, I'm going to take half of the sandwich." Each of us would claim what we wanted to eat. Out of the three lunches, we would have our breakfast.

We would run and let them play tag and everybody knew where to meet up at the end, so we could eat it up really fast before school started. These kids would be out there running around looking for their lunches and we had already eaten them. We would go to class and we would be full. We had to do this because we were poor, and they didn't have the free breakfast and lunch program going on at that particular time.

One day, they made an announcement over the P.A. system about how you need to watch out, because a lot of children's lunches are coming up missing. But the lunches never came up missing until we got there.

* * *

After they tore down the house on Roselawn, we moved to Henry Gardens projects, which was on Joy Road. We attended the Henry Gardens Elementary School. At the Henry Gardens projects, there was always something to do, but we never had all these little different things, because like I said, dad was always strung out and he knew how to get in contact with the dope fiends that were in the area no matter where we moved.

It was a habitat for drugs and things in the Henry Garden projects. He still tried to work off and on, although, it was a hard life, he still kept us. He would give us different tips; different game, and we would see different ways in dealing with different people, but we had to learn how to adjust ourselves and be invisible kids at the same time. We were well versed in surviving the streets.

Sometimes I wonder if all of us lived in the same house, because some of us did the same thing that we saw and seem to somewhat enjoy it. They were helpless. I am not putting anyone down because I cannot point any fingers. If I point one finger at you, I'm pointing three back at me, so what have I done? What am I doing?

Because of how I grew up, I learned earlier in life, at a young age, how to like myself. When we lived in the Henry Garden projects, it was a rough life. In spite of it, we would play hockey, football, and we would entertain each other. For instance, when the TV was broken, the one little radio Ronald couldn't fix, or we couldn't find a battery, we still found a way to entertain one another. We knew every song that came on the radio, we knew how to play marbles, Mother-may-I, hide-n'-seek, jump rope, anything; racing, anything, you name it. We could do it. It was more or less a part of our surviving technique.

Sometimes outside we would play football and the other kids would have on football gear; the helmet, the shoulder pads, the whole nine yards, the spikes, and we would be out there with coats on, smelling funky and tearing them up, Jack! While we were playing football we would lose our shoes and things because we were enthralled in the game.

I would hate to get something new. I used to hate to get something new; I hated for my Father to buy anything new. Although he wasn't paying that much for rent, with all us kids, we would have little clothes and food, but he had to take care of that habit.

When he bought us something new, we would get a whipping. I'm like, damn, I don't want him to buy me anything new man, *don't buy me nothing*--I'll go out here and hustle and buy my own things, that's what we did mostly. *Don't buy me nothing new*, because if he bought us something worth $2.50 from Farmer Foods, Yankees or anywhere else in Detroit, we got an ass whipping before you put it on. While he was whipping us, he told us don't tear it up. Now have you, these shoes was called "Slip n' Slides". These shoes will tear up if you look at them too hard, and *goddamnit*, excuse me. If you don't believe me, I would tear them up in one week. I had to drag my feet around until I got outside. Then when we get outside, I let them flip and flap. In other words, the shoes would do their own thing. Then he'll notice them after he come out of a long nod, after about two or three months later, he'll notice them.

He would say, "How you tear them *goddam* shoes up, you want to get your ass whipped again?!!!" *Buy me some good shoes then*, this is what I am saying to myself and I'd have that look on my face, and he'll say, "You know, I can't stand you."

I used to get my ass whipped for everything, because when he asked me a question, I'm the type that wasn't trying to humor him. I was just trying to answer the question. And it didn't bother me, I knew I was going to get a whippin', but it didn't bother me.

I was singled out, I took the burden; the blame of a lot of things that happened and my brothers and sisters would just blame things on me because they know he didn't like me. They would always say, "Ricky did it." Every time something happened, "Ricky did it." "Ricky did it." I was taught earlier in life that I was going to be lied on.

I did things that were different, and I would never tell my pops what I was doing. I did things to better myself and be invisible. I would hustle so that I could purchase my own shoes. I would go to the thrift store and find some nice things.

I would do anything in my power to try to be invisible and find places to go, like the Salvation Army. At the Salvation Army it would be a number of us that would make pottery statue heads and skeletons during the holidays, we would paint them, and these would be Christmas presents. There were Wood Shop classes that we would take or something of that nature, and we'd make different types of birds. This is what we did with our hands because we could not afford to buy presents.

Our focus with our money was to buy food for one another, even if it was only some rice and butter.

CHAPTER THREE

One year our Grandmother came up and while we were living in the projects, she asked us the year before what did we want for Christmas. We asked for a radio because we liked to dance, sing, and entertain our friends. By this time, we were in the Herman Garden Elementary School in Detroit. During our lunch period the school allowed us to dance and we could bring records to play. We also had a little, you know, a *boom box*, with the little box in front of it. It had a little handle with a sound system that bounced off the walls in the house.

This is how we would have our parties. My sister would get the little 45's from the store. This is when they had 45's. A group of them would go to Yankees and shoplift the 45's that they had on the table and we would keep up with them. We would listen to the tune on the radio. We knew every dance because we lived out there. We would practice dance steps, just like you do today. Most of the kids know more about these dances and the songs than they did about education.

We would have so much fun at Herman Garden Projects. We would dance and skate at Herman Garden

Projects Elementary School Hall. We would have house parties. We'd sell hot-dogs for about a quarter, potato chips for a dime, and we'd get a couple of pops and sell them for a dime. This is how we made a little extra cash.

The money we made at our parties would go straight for the old man's habit, but we were able to get around it and keep some money for ourselves. The blue strobe light would make us feel like dancing as soon as we walked into the party. Some parents would be there to chaperone us. We really had fun, literally, poor but having fun.

We went to visit Chicago during one Christmas holiday season, we were brought up to Chicago, now have you, the old man will get us out of Detroit every now and then, and you know, even though we got there on a wing and a prayer, the car would break down as soon as we got there. One of his buddies would get us down there and then … would jump off.

* * *

There was one incident when we were little, one time we were living in Cleveland, there was a bank robbery; we were living on Lynnwood, and we were at school. The police came and pulled all of us out of class. They interrogated us about a bank robbery. We had no knowledge of the bank robbery, but they felt that we did. They started asking us questions like: did we have any money? Did we see a lot of money? Is there money in our house? And so on and so forth.... We answered, "No *ain't* no money in our house, the school had to give us underwear and stuff." Because we smelled really bad and our underwear was all tore up.

We would wear our underwear until they turn into a skirt, the bottom would be gone, but you know, the rubber part would last the longest, the bottom was the gray dirty part that just hung there. Those were our underwear. So and um, when you're poor, really poor, like we were, like a lot of people are today, you have a certain smell about yourselves. It's a dirty, pee, musty smell. Everyone in the community almost had the same smell.

The mentality in our community was very poor. While we were living on Wade Park, we met some girls that lived up there. One of their names was Phyllis, along with her sister. They were a little bit older than us. We had to be like six years old or somewhere between there, five or six. These girls were real fast, but they were church-going girls. They taught us more mature things about life.

For us to be so poor, we still had fun. We would invent fun. We had to be creative. Not like the children nowadays. Doctors prescribing Thorazine and Lithium to treat psychotic and bipolar children, and tell children that they are educationally and mentally handicapped, but we as a people tend to learn things real fast, especially if we're taught. We can learn it. Nowadays the kids can't even go out and play and have fun and venture out and make things because the violence on the street is so dangerous.

When they get to school there is more room than a little apartment that they may live in, and they tend to cut up, because there is room to run around. They don't get to go outside and wander far away from the house like we were able to do when we were smaller.

The doctor would wonder why we're still happy when we don't have anything. What sense does it make to be sad and poor? There's no need in being poor and sad. We didn't really realize that we were poor because we became accustom to it. There were times we recognized it, but we played it off—it didn't really bother us.

I had a friend who had a mini-bike and he owned a lot of toys. He would let me ride on the back. His name was John Montgomery. One day somebody took his mini-bike and it was just a mess. He got very upset and didn't want to play for a short while.

The old man would be up and down sometimes. Sometimes he would be in the box. What used to trip me out is how game recognizes game. I didn't understand how, and the way I'm seeing it today, most of these young brothers, they are the DOCTORS at the beginning, they distribute the medicine, the drugs, the habits and things, then they end up being the patient. Till this day, I do not understand it. Now if you're the DOCTOR, how do you end up being the patient? That means you got slicked by the slickest. The DOCTORS did not realize being around it and touching the medicine can make you addicted to it. Then you want to take it to the next level and use the medicine and become your best customer.

Our Father told us when we get in trouble he didn't like to go up to school because he had tracks on his arms, so you know teachers might have noticed them. We tried our best not to involve our Father when we got in trouble.

We were exposed to all this at an early age, and I don't knock it, gay or lesbian. I don't knock none of this because that's not my business because it's like I say, I can't point the finger. They have to deal with that lifestyle themselves. I was taught by all of them. I mean, I never had to do anything like that. You had to have some common sense, and you had to learn how to play the game.

When we were younger, it was against the law to be a *sissy*—they didn't really say too much about lesbians, I don't think it was against the law to be a dope fiend only if you got caught. So, you know, you had to keep things undercover, keep it under wraps.

We also learned how to drive at an early age, because we used to drive the old man around because he could only see through one eye and had bad feet. He used to like to take us around because we had a little game about ourselves.

As we were growing older, I used to always watch people I watched the mistakes they made and tried not to make those same mistakes. Why would I have to do the same things that you're doing in order to prove myself? Why re-invent the wheel. This is the way it was.

Going to school, I understood things that other kids didn't understand because that's the way our lifestyle was. It was real fast, very aggressive. It was *do* or die in the making.

We got put out of the Herman Garden Projects, because our Father wouldn't pay the rent. My old man didn't really like paying any kind of rent, so the state put us in another house. Even though the state put us in this big house, I still don't know until this day how we got in this house, it was a really nice big house on Chicago Avenue in Detroit, Michigan right off of Rivera. We transferred to a new school called Rudderman & Cody.

Rudderman & Cody was real prejudice. It was a Junior high school, so at this time we were going there and we used to have to walk a long way to get there, but we got there. At the same time it was kind of hard because we were watching King get killed, Martin Luther King that is ... there were riots. At the time we were living in Cleveland.

People were very upset so they started burning down buildings, so we went to church to stay safe. There was a church called Calvary. They would have arts and crafts, make key chains, and give us small Easter and Thanksgiving baskets. They would give us parties and offer us little goody bags because we were poor. During the summer, we would attend the daycare camp. They would serve us small ice cream cups for dessert. They would teach us songs, *Yes Jesus Loves Me* and all these regular Bible songs. We were happy and this made the priests of the church look good. We enjoyed it so much that we made sure we didn't miss going. We learned how to make chains and had developed skills in crafting.

While living on Nichols, it was an old folk's home behind us, and they called it the Tract Garden. The Tract Garden had this big old piece of land where we used to go to catch grasshoppers, act silly, and have fun. They came up with the idea one day to have all the little children plant seeds to grow a garden of vegetables. Before we could plant, they had us plow by digging the land and turning the dirt over. We were organized and set out our garden plots.

Our job was to get up early in the morning, and till the land using hoes and rakes, in order to keep the weeds down from around the vegetables. We grew carrots, corn, tomatoes and a number of different fruits and vegetables. We could take some home with us when they were ripe. We watched them grow from nothing into something.

After the fruit and vegetables matured, they took them into the old folk's home and used them for their meals. During the night, we would get up and go over to the garden and grab a couple of carrots and rinse them off to eat by climbing the fence because we were hungry.

In Detroit we used to organize talent shows, just to entertain ourselves. We made something out of nothing, it was life. At that time, even before then, when the old man had got out of jail again, we were introduced to the Nation of Islam, the Honorable Elijah Muhammad. We had the star and the moon on the wall. Although the old man came in for a few minutes, he disappeared again. He had already been in jail, and I guess Muslim were around when he got there so they practice Islam.

We watched King, Malcolm X, and John F. Kennedy get assassinated. During that time, we were going through a little self-recognition ourselves, we were moving up. We also watched the Vietnam War. This was also during the time we lived in Cleveland when our old man got shot in the backyard as I mentioned earlier. This was during the time I was at a tender age … I was around three or four years old, I don't even think I was in school at that particular time, if I'm not mistaken.

While we were watching television, we saw on the news a sister we knew named, Alfreda Robison's mother who shot her brother for hollering at the kids, she didn't know he was on drugs. He was the one that taught us some Black Panther moves, along with Karate. That is when we were coming out with: "We the People," "More power to the People," "No power to the Pig." We were blackness.

She shot her brother dead right there in the street, right in front of us, we watched him die not realizing it was going to be aired on the news. This had just been a violent set for us while we were coming up. We still were able to function and make the best out of a bad situation.

When we moved in the house on Chicago Avenue in Detroit, Michigan, I don't know what happened. Like I say, one day we were just sitting there, the old man came in frantic, telling us to get everything together and let's get out of here. So, we really took what was on our backs, we took the truck, and from there, we ended up here in Chicago with some relatives that didn't expect us.

When we got to Chicago, we stayed with Aunt Alice, she stayed on Fillmore. The building is still there, just one of the few buildings that still exist. Like I said earlier every other building we lived in has been torn down, but from what I understand, the house on Chicago Avenue is still there.

I don't think that Nichol, Wade Park and all the other places are still there. Most of them have been torn down – the house on 14th Street and Springfield is gone and a couple more of the other buildings are gone or they've been condemned and some people are just in it and they're just there.

The one on Central Park and Monroe is gone. Mostly every building that we lived in has been torn down which were condemned places in the first place.

The worn walls full of cracks and holes with the few wooden planks lined horizontally with white dust of drywall sporadically on each board as I gaze into every room shaking my head slowly back and forth of the destruction of our living condition. Wooden floors creaking with every step we take with pieces of wood sticking up throughout every vertical board causing us to walk as if we are stepping on a landmine being careful not to get a splinter in our feet. Toilets filled with corrosion in the bowl and around the stool especially along the base that is attached to the floor. I looked at the cracked bathroom mirror door to the medicine cabinet, afraid to open it because the pieces of glass might shatter and cut me. The sink and bathtub grew fungus that is black and green. The kitchen was dark and gray with many invisible souls crying out for food because of hunger. You can feel the presence of the old souls that dwelled in here screaming for a way out of this condition. Dust that had settled for years was waking up and filling the air with a thick gray haze as we toured the abandon apartment.

Is this where we are going to be living while our Father was in a room preparing his dope to shoot? It never seemed to brother him as long as he was able to take his medicine.

Before walking into the condemned buildings our eyes scan the neighborhood looking at the deprived condition on the right and to the left of us. The dirt in front of each brick layered building moved from one area to another as the wind blew creating designs in the air. When the wind stopped blowing, some of the dirt didn't fall to the ground it attached itself to our clothes and body as if we were wearing it like a layer of clothing.

We saw sequels flying around as if they were looking for dead corpses. This place was old, dark and glooming. No one in their right mind would even drive down this street with only one street light that would come on at night

We learned how to swim at an early age, so we swam in the lagoon. We used to make fishing rods out of a stick and out of a safety pin and catch little fish and we would cook them. We used to hang around Lee) Park; they had a swimming pool where we swam also.

Jim Brown, the football player played for the Cleveland Browns. Jim used to live somewhere near Lee Park. We went around there one time and he was beating up his girlfriend. During this era, it was what some men did – beat their women.

CHAPTER FOUR

When I went to a school called Henrotin Rigkin it was located on Homan Avenue. This was during the time we were going through a lot of drama: our Mother's death, our Father's addiction, and moving from place to place. We were just a mess. We were a balled up mess. We were trying to adjust to our situation and our new environment.

When the principal told me that I needed to go to a different school, I went and told my Father what he had said. Although my Father never went up to schools for us, he went this time to get my transfer as the school insisted.

I asked questions about the school, when I got there. I just didn't feel right. The school didn't look right—it just didn't. This school was just going to make me out of a failure, if at all possible. No one graduated out of Henrotin Rigkin elementary school, but you know, this was like you were not on your way to high school anyway.

I was almost in eighth grade. I thought about an uncle who had a house on 13th and Troy name Luke David. Since I did not want to attend Henrotin Rigkin, I did not turn in any of the paperwork and decided to use my Uncle's address so that I could get into Hess Upper Grade Center.

The teachers at Hess Upper Grade Center taught me well and answered all the questions I asked. Not like Henrotin who put me down and said I was dumb just because I did not take a lot of mess off of anyone. I wasn't a bully but if you took me there, I went there and took care of business. We lived in a violent environment. I wasn't violent unless you were violent with me—and then I took care of my business—you want to play, let's play; I had nothing to lose.

I had a lot of anger built up inside of me for years of being deprived. I still learned how to shove it off and focus on what was important and that was surviving.

I eventually transferred over to Hess Upper Grade Center; they would accept the school work I turned in because I was able to explain what I was trying to do, it might not have come out in the writing part, but I was able to explain it to them. Now they call this learning disability dyslexia. I would probably be diagnosed with dyslexia now; if they were to test me.

I would always constantly be degraded by others telling me that I am not this or that and was put down. It would somewhat destroy my self-esteem. I would still say if you put me next to a genius, I would run rings around them and they know it.

It was just like the infamous: "Willie Lynch Letter". If you ever get a chance to get it, read it. The "Willie Lynch Letter" reveals the trickery that has been going on for years and years, until this day we are still going, we can stand here for 400 years to a thousand, the way it looks the man is still getting his thousand out us.

I was able to graduate from Hess during a time when the condemned buildings were being torn down. A group of us during our spare time had a couple of hammers and we started stacking bricks because we weren't in school during the summer. When we made a little money, they cheated us out of our money because we were younger than the older people, but they gave the older folks their money.

We stacked those bricks just as good as anybody else. Stacking bricks was an art. You would pick up a brick and knock off the mortar and then stack them. The buildings in Chicago were deteriorating so the city would have bulldozers knock them down one by one and then someone had to go and recover the bricks. We knocked the mortar off until the brick was clean and smooth.

We would then take the other end, if we had any chips, we just scrubbed them off and then stacked them up very neatly into a big square and then they would spray them, mark them, seal, and then we should have gotten paid about five dollars a stack, but they were giving us a dollar fifty cents per stack. Then you know, once we did that we had a little something to eat.

One of our Aunts used to work at the school, she used to bring home old lunchroom cookies, some milk that would be spoiled, and cereal, but we were still able to function. We were able to eat something; because the old man had ran back and forth to Detroit, and she was getting tired of us and getting tired of him; he didn't give her any money and she was scared of all of us because she was getting old at this time.

I understand, you know, and we made our Aunt nervous, but she knew to take us places with her because she felt safe with us. She used to sleep with a manikin in her bed to make it seem like it was somebody there just in case somebody came in on her, they would think it was a man in the house. This is what she would tell us.

The Aunt that worked at the school had a hair salon in Cleveland; she styled my sister Regina's hair. She then traveled from Cleveland to Chicago with Aunt Bea, Aunt Doll and Aunt Willa-Mae. These people did well for themselves. Including Uncle Percy; all of them did well, and Uncle Jessie, coming from Mississippi and wherever else they had come from, including Cleveland.

Then our Aunt put us out, we moved to a building, on 14th & Springfield, which was almost condemned, we used to always have to keep it clean for our Father, and this is how we paid our portion of the rent.

Because the old man, by him having so many kids, he was able to get by. A lot of times the police wanted to take him to jail, but he had so many kids, the DCFS program wasn't in at that particular time, they gave him a break because of all of the kids he had. But he was always into something and he always had something going on.

The old man was able to lie in bed with two women at a time, sometimes three, whatever way he wanted to do, he was a player and they loved him, they liked him-they would do anything he says and they would never fight each other and when they did, he whipped both of them. I would wonder to myself sometimes why, when this guy was sleep, why they didn't just beat him to death. He had some kind of game, the gift of gab, but whatever he had, they liked it; they really liked it.

We were so exposed to the street life that we would watch them mix the Dope with Dorums, they would get them with the Heroin, they would go buy these Dorum pills, open them up and spread them out and put the brown dope on it, the Heroin, and mix it up and put it in bags, they would stretch it. They might buy a "Spoon of -P-", that's what they called it and they would take that *Spoon of -P-,* that might cost them about five hundred dollars for that spoon, and they come out with about eight hundred dollars out of it. The old man was going to get his share out of it.

He prepared the hit, *bard-it* making it already when they got it, they called it hit and *stepped on,* and they stepped on it again as long as you got your little nod out of it, you were good to go. We watched them mix it up, cook it; and tie up with the syringe-needle going into their arm, some of them would shoot in their legs, some of them would shoot in their necks, some of them would even shoot in their private section because they had used up all of their veins.

My old man had got so bad that his veins dried up; they were so hard, they called him "Ropes", when you use up all your veins, and the veins in your hands and everywhere, then he would shoot in his neck, if he would've did anything wrong, he would've killed himself. He used to have to put his two fingers in his mouth and blow until his jaws swell spider veins pop into his neck and he let one of his friends hit him. Then some of the guys had got so bad that when--they had used up every vein in their body they had to "*skin pop*", we call it skin pop, most of them that you see they would be swollen up, the whole body would be swollen up, except the head-it be this big swollen man with an itty bitty head, because the Dope was messing them up. Then they got so bad, they had taken the Dope off the set and they were giving them Methadone.

The Methadone program talking about you were going to kill--but that's when the Dope was drying up and you had to be on something in order to keep this *sick* off you. The Heroin was so bad that it just knock you down, you can't move, you don't want to function, you'd kill anything to get to it. They did the same thing in Vietnam; gave the brothers that dope and stuff and then they would--I can understand, you would be just totally mad-you're sick, you're mad—you're sick, you're mad, you'd do anything in order to get this little *Jones*, and then they'll come out there and try to keep you calm and send a little bit more out there for you, so that's how we got a lot of drug addicts in the system.

Now this is the Government have you, doing all of this too. I was able to watch all of this, and it was just a mad set man-it's a mad set. I'm throwing these little hints that I want you to remember and take something out of it because it's not just a story of life; it's a story of light. If you do this right, you'll be surprised at how you will reach the route of passage without any complaints, and you'll be able to function and understand. You learned to like yourself and love yourself. All these people that have been going through the Dope *thang*, and we watched all this as we grew up, I mean, this happened while we were little.

While we were sitting there, we'd be watching them shoot Dope and he'd reach over and knock the shit out of me; "Fuck you looking at, you want to shoot some motherfucking Dope, motherfucker!" "You want to shoot some Dope; you want to shoot this shit motherfucker! You want some of this?" He would break a pistol out and put it in my face, you understand, cock a shotgun, put it in my face, and all that shit, and then he'd put the gun in my hand while he got a shotgun and tell me to pull the trigger. "You thinking about killing me, motherfucker; that's what you doing, you thinking about killing me motherfucker, that's what you thinking about?! Shoot me motherfucker, shoot me! Shoot that motherfucking gun!, that's what you...." And then I would hold the gun down wouldn't want to shoot.... "I said shoot it motherfucker! If you don't shoot it, I'm gone shoot your motherfucking ass!" And he got the gun; got the shotgun upside my head, I'm still not scared or nothing, but I'm like, *this motherfucker is crazy*, so I shoot the gun in the house.

He says, "So now you see what a motherfucking gun sound like, what a motherfucking gun will do motherfucker!" You know what a motherfucking gun will do, it will kill a motherfucker!" "If you ever pull a gun on a motherfucker, motherfucker, you better kill them, you understand me, motherfucker!"

I'm going through this; I'm going through this-shit. I get my ass whipped, wake up in the morning, get my ass whipped; go to bed at night, get my ass whipped. But after all this ass whippin', it was considered as love. That's spooky *ain't* it? That's real scary; after you've been going through all this drama, you done seen all this abuse throughout your life and this is all you've been introduced to, you accepted this as love; you wanted to get hit-you wanted to get whipped-although I didn't. But some of them do, it looked like they did anyway, but I just got my ass whipped because I was trying to be invisible. Trying to stay out of his way and learn the game. When people used to OD (overdose) in our household, or fall out because they used to do *thangs* ... it was my job to bring them back to life.

You suppose to push on their heart and walk them around, and stuff like that, but I'd hit you in your motherfucking chest and get that motherfucker thumping back. I was like, I hit so motherfucking hard, I'd make your heart start beating. By the time I hit you, you'd stand, what? What? And then they could walk, and when they start walking, we'd walk you out the motherfucking house. Sometimes I would try to walk them through the house in the summertime....

Now these brothers with this new Dope right now, instead of trying to keep you alive, walking you, keeping you iced, they just let you die. We had to ice the old man a whole bunch of times, about three times, he almost checked out of here with that Dope.

We used to walk him, ice him up, and keep him up for a long time until he came back, milking him and things of this nature. But the brother that's on this new Dope right now, they be hitting the pipe and they fall out or whatever they're doing, they get on this shit right now, instead of trying to help you and bring you back, these brothers want to--they grab the pipe and leave you there. There's no honor among dope fiends no more, no game.

CHAPTER FIVE

GAME ON THE STREET

When we played Three Card Monte, we had a group of us working together in order to convince others that they could win some money. They had to play in order to win. Another game is when you were on an airplane where you had this TV box and it was nothing but bricks in it, and you tell somebody you just sold it and you have your friend dress up in a police uniform, as if he is the security guard, and he's looking for you and they got to hurry up and give you the money, and they drive off and when they get home they go home and open the box and find they got bricks.

We used to do the paper chase, you know, when they tell you they found this money and you had to put some money with this and would convince you that was safe, then they tied it up in this little handkerchief and give it to you. Once you walk around the corner with it, they would do a switch on you. A pickpocket would bump into you and steal the money. You would come out of it with nothing. By the time you find out, they are gone with the paper chase.

The selling of the syrup: The syrup is like cough syrup, along with Codeine pills, mixed together called hooch which would put you in a nod; it was a cool high for folks, you're sleep but you're awake. You could crunch the pills and mix it with cough syrup called shake and bake. While you were high off of hooch, you would be very thirsty. This was sold right on the street even though it was prescription medicine.

Then it got so bad, they started doing T's- & Blues, we call them T-shirts and Blue Jeans, T's and Blues, or whatever you want to call it. They would crush these pills up, snort it, and they would crush them up and shoot them. Everybody started shooting T's & Blues. At first they were fifty cents. When the dope man started selling them, you used to get them for fifty cents. Now they're five dollars. Dope fiends could use them in place of Heroin, that's how fast the market is for them, they set their own prices for them.

A long time ago, when you started shooting T's & Blues, they'd lock you up, make you handicap, but they still kept shooting the T's & Blues through a needle. They started cooking this shit up like they would cook up some Heroin and things. They did the same thing with T's & Blues, found out it was locking up a lot of them, making them paraplegic, just taking them out of here.

These people have been sissies and dope fiends for all these years, not until just recently, you're just hearing about AIDS. They either put something on the Dope, or it was programmed to go like this. All I'm asking the dope fiends that are getting high; pay attention to what's happening; you're sitting here smoking ready rock rock cocaine, it's all they've been introduced to, you see how fast it's taking you out of here. Don't you think it's something on this dope? This shit been out here a long time ago. As I mentioned earlier, how these drugs can take them out and how they're still using them. Once you are hooked, it is very difficult to stop using.

* * *

You know I was speaking earlier about how they tried to put me in the Learning Disability Class when I was coming up. This is nothing but a conspiracy to destroy black boys and men. I also was talking about how they destroyed the black family again in the late fifties, early sixties, when they gave the black woman ADC (Aide for Dependent Children) and the black man had to hide or leave the house when the caseworker came out to the house.

Sometimes our Father would be there and he would have to stay around and we would call him Uncle Ricky. Even when she had her boyfriend, it would be the same thing--we would call him Uncle Ricky; this is another way of degrading yourself and bringing yourself down, and although, they're doing this here today. But out of all the times that I was living with my Father, and I was being treated badly at the same time, it taught me game. It taught me how to be strong, it taught me how to take care of my business-when I say take care of my business, it kept me out of jail.

I will discuss the jail situation later in the book. If you ever pull a gun on a person, you better use it--take care of your business. You were able to see the drug game and see if you really wanted to be in it. We were checking trap at an early age around thirteen and fourteen. We were out there checking trap for the old man; with our hair processed. I was driving at 13.

When I say check trap, trap is like when you have some whores ("hoes"), the *hoes* that they would have out on the street, they weren't always the old man's *hoes*, it might be some of the slick guys or people that would come over to the house, by them liking me, they would call themselves teaching me and taking me up under their arms.

You know, I was able to have a pistol on me and things like this in order to protect the *hoes* and myself. You weren't going to jail because you were just a teenager. And when we got up to Chicago, gang banging had slowed down a little bit. It had got real, it had really slowed down, they were still gang banging, just like they are now, but it had slowed down.

When we were leaving Detroit, some of the people that were there, some of my friends that had heard about Chicago, said that they were going to make us pierce our ears and make us join a gang; and we were like, no they *ain't* gone make us do this, uh un, not me man--but now I got four holes in my ears, and I still haven't had to be in a gang.

Like I was saying, all that drama and all that abuse that we went through, we thought it was love. At the same time, what I did, I would step out of myself every day, even back then, and look at how my day went, what happened? What was the good and bad part of it? And also, I would watch those that were involved in these situations, to see how well they were doing. They weren't doing well at all. They would be up for a minute and then they'd be down the next.

The only way the old man stayed out of jail is because he had us. DCFS hadn't kicked in yet. It got to be degrading when your woman got the money and you didn't have any money which creates a hostile environment. It is called divide and conquer.

The black family was doing well before all the riots and stuff. We would get out and we would make a living, we would make an earning for ourselves and things like that, but when they introduced ADC, it destroyed the black family. It took the male figure out of the house. Although, if you go back; we never went in the house too tough anyway.

In my opinion, we were used for study and things like that. Check out our history. This is what I would be thinking about as I was going through my life! Why is this? How is this?

While living in Detroit, we were still living and had a good time even though we were poor. We would play Jacks for hours at a time, Bat-'n-Ball, Hula Hoop; we would play Tag, Dodge Ball, and we also made Go-karts, we made some of the *baddest* go-karts you could ever see.

We made one that looked just like a rocket ship; you'd think some professionals made it. We had a steering wheel on it; we put springs on it to make it come back and forth to us, like it had power steering, had a stick on it for the brakes. We even put a little back compartment on it for the person that would push the go-kart. He could sit down when we go really fast, he could go for the ride also. It had to have balance; it had to have some kind of stability to it. We did it without an instructional manual. No one taught us how to do this; we just did it because we had nails and wood, wheels, a steering wheel and a pole; and we just put this thing together. We had fun!

Kids now-a-days don't even know how to even do this; parents have to buy it, they have to buy them a little electric car in the store. They gotta have the best bikes; they gotta have everything that comes out of a manufacturer's box. Sometimes we need to step back on certain things and allow our children to use their brains to come up with creating things.

When we were in Detroit, it was rough, as I said before, but we used whatever was available to us. People would look at us with an expression on their face that says, "How in the hell are they still happy?" Because we weren't trying anything else, this is what we would call happy.

I had an Uncle named Billy, he was with the O'Jays. He could play every instrument you could imagine. He could sing and dance. When we were living in Cleveland, he had brought us all kinds of instruments, Congas, Bongos, a Flute, a Guitar, a Piano and a couple more little instruments. I still remember the Trumpets he introduced to us. Even till this day, I collect instruments. If you come to my house now, you'll find a piano, a violin, a flute, a clarinet, a trombone, congas, er, er, er, a guitar; you know, some type of instrument to keep the kids busy.

Several times the old man had messed up the dope man's money; we got chased up here to Chicago and the family was doing badly. Ronald and Regina left me with the other kids. I would work at night and go to school in the daytime, take me a few little clothes there because I took care of the old man, his habit, I dressed him; we were teenagers, my old man, he was an adult, he would be dressed like I was dressed, like he was a teenager. He thought it was cool even when the platform shoes came out, he wore the platform shoes. He got mad, but he had to wear them because those were the ones I bought. And he would wear my pants and my shirts and stuff and swear he was clean and I would go out and start buying gangster hats and *things* because at this time, while we were in Detroit and Chicago, we got a chance to look at Superfly and the Mack; everybody wanted to be Superfly and the Mack—everybody-everybody.

This is during the time we came out of that Heroin *thang* and started messing with the Cocaine. Everybody wanted to mess with Cocaine, but the old man stayed with the Heroin for a long time, till they took it off the streets for a while.

While attending Manley High School, I was functioning every day because I was able to eat twice a day. I was around fifteen years old. Boys at school were fighting me taking my money creating a lot of drama in my life. The old man wanted me to stop fighting because every time I was involved in a fight, the school would report it to my Father.

He would constantly tell me that I ain't shit. I heard this all my life, and I wasn't going to be shit. He said that I was going to be dead before I turned nineteen years old; this is what he would tell me. I was the only one that was really afraid to steal, even to this day, I don't like to steal. I don't like to lie. I sometimes get in trouble because I won't lie. I didn't lie then and I shouldn't have to lie now. I was constantly told how I was dumb and stupid. It affected me, but I found something else to do. I can show you better than I can tell you.

Every game that I was involved in be it physical, mental, sexual, or whatever, you paid for the game, okay, believe me, whoever played the game had to pay for the game. The game on the street is fair, that's right I said it, it's fair in war and all, for those that's coming up, when you get mad and upset and frustrated you have to play the game by the rules in order to play fair.

I used to hate to see my old man coming, I used to hate it and I didn't understand it. I would hold that hate in, but I never went off and hit him or *raised* up and just totally disrespected him, but as I got older I would have him stop doing the things that he would do by the words that I would say. I would use language or what you would call Standard English and he would back off. He would always say, "Ask me if I give a fuck." He really didn't, I have that attitude to a certain extent too; "Ask me if I give a fuck." The answer is: no I don't. I don't give a fuck about what you think about me.

*   *   *

Now, DCFS is coming into play. A caseworker came and saw how rough we lived. It was really bad. I asked my Uncle Luke who was a school teacher if I could stay with him. I told him that I would do chores by keeping the house clean, wash the cars, and sweep the hallway. He thought it would be a great idea, so he let me come and stay with him. I did whatever he asked me to do. We had running water, and I didn't have to worry about food.

Aunt Bea stayed upstairs from Uncle Luke. I recall going flipping back and forth from upstairs and downstairs - from one apartment to another until eventually she died.

I explained to my Uncle why I was so illiterate as far as my reading and English. Because of my Father's lifestyle, I was from the street. This was during the time I was in my sophomore year. I refused to give up and just quite.

When living with my Father, he told me that I didn't have to work or go to school. He would make us stay home to chase the mailman for his check. Sometimes the check wouldn't come until four days later. While waiting, we had to miss school. Our job was to tell our Father when we saw the mailman coming. At this time, we would be missing school; I didn't need to miss school because that was a meal and plus, I was missing lessons and what the teacher was teaching. I was so illiterate that I couldn't do the basics. I didn't have *no* business missing *no* school.

Once I started living with Uncle Luke, life got better for me. I started dressing and looking good. I was dressing like the ghetto people dressed. You got whatever was poppin' for that time or whatever the style was. Once I got introduced to dressing, you know, I would buy fine clothes from nice stores. Uncle Luke taught me how to budget my money.

When you came up with the old man, you weren't talking about a checking account, a bank book, paying taxes; paying your gas, light or telephone bill, and how much this one cost and how much that one cost, or how to look through the paper and find sales on certain things that you need and then buy it -- soap, deodorant, anything -- little minor things. You didn't have information on things, so when I was introduced to it, it was a whole *nother* world; I had to start all over again like a new born baby.

Uncle Luke had already experienced this, and he introduced it to me but he couldn't teach me how to read, he couldn't teach me to read, couldn't teach me to count. I was in my sophomore year he had to play catch-up for real. He was the one that suggested that I go to Evelyn Woods reading school. He tried everything in his power to help.

What my hang-up was in regards to reading was, I used to read for the old man, and we used to go to the library and try to get some books and do a little different stuff like homework. But the old man--if I missed a word or didn't know a word, he would beat me so bad that when I saw a book, I would just start sweating; when I saw words, I would just start sweating; I couldn't even function, I just remember the ass whippin' I'm gone get if I miss one word.

A book was used as a weapon. It was used as ... I saw a book as something that was dangerous, something that would get you hurt from knowing it. But now I see a book as wisdom, knowledge and understanding. I mean, I can go through them like pancakes. You can't keep me away from a book. I always have something on hand to read now; always. And I'm constantly learning, 24 hours a day I learn, learn, and learn. Now, I can teach what I learn.

This is why they keep books away from you all. Because once you start picking up books and reading them, you find out that he writes a lot of stuff and keeps records of what we do, because he is part of this conspiracy to destroy us. And then if you don't reach the route of passage, you can't function.

If we never have been taught how to be a man, then you don't know how to be a man. If you're there with just your mother, she can just teach you certain things, but you must have that father image. You cannot teach a girl how to become a woman and vice-versa.

If you were treated badly by your mother and your father, why would you inflict this same pain on someone else? The way you were raised gets seared in your mind. If your mom treats you bad, then you might treat women bad. If you are a girl and your dad treats you bad, you might treat guys bad. Because we lived with it for so many years, to us it might be normal. I was looking at, all that abuse, and the hardship that I went through. I didn't like it; so why would I inflict this on other little kids or anybody else that was coming up? I couldn't do it, see the bucks stopped here, the buck has always stopped here.

It still has stopped here. I *ain't* mad, I *ain't* trying to get on one of these little talk shows with a victim card. Like I say, I can show you better than I can tell you. And I'm showing you now through the information inside this book and what I've become today.

I was living much better. DCFS took my brothers and sisters and put them in foster homes. They were able to attend the same school. This is another form of embarrassment. I watched them go there and my Father was over there. Even till this day, we are just like friends, my brothers and sisters and I. We see each other when we can, and when we do, it might be at a funeral, or I might bump into them at a skating rink or something like that, or I just stop by and see them.

My siblings and I would treat each other, even on the street, like friends. When I say friends, it's not too personal. Whatever their style is or whatever they like doing, that's their world; you don't knock it-that's theirs.

We would help one another, but we *ain't* gon' keep helping you on the same problem because you lived in the same environment, came out at the same time we did. I had to grow up fast. I never was a kid, never was able to live as a kid. I was always grown from the time I was born.

Now we have an understanding where we're not jealous of each other, or hate each other or hold any animosity towards one another because one is doing better. We also watched that in my Father's family. They were so busy trying to outdo each other that they couldn't come together. When they did come together, they hid what they were going through because they were going through drama before they got there. This could have been passed on from generation to generation.

This was not a mistake. As we were going through the system, they put my siblings in foster homes. My brother David couldn't stay there because he was a year younger than me. He had already been taking care of himself and all of a sudden he has to go by these rules, and he had to go to this church and do all this other stuff. We were introduced to church, like I mentioned earlier, we were introduced to Islam; we were introduced to the Baptist church; and the Christian church. We always had some kind of faith in our lives.

I also was going to church when my Mother died and I had got so upset I felt God was punishing us when she died. This caused me to start studying the Bible after asking the question, "Why?" Then I started listening to what people were saying but I didn't have an understanding. It would be different just from what I heard.

We were able to comprehend things a lot quicker and faster than other kids did and that was a blessing for me, and that's how I got through high school, I was able to listen, not just hear you, I was able to listen to what you say and give you an answer to your question. You would say, "There's something different about this kid." I could talk to adults better than I could kids. I never was a kid. I had a little kid body, a little kid head, but I never was a kid. And when we were little, we used to talk about each other something terrible. They used to call me muscle head, living lower lip. They used to call my other brother David, Motown, because he had a mole on the back of his head. We called my brother Ronald Turtle because he moved slowly. Regina, just was, we used to call her Mrs. Bea, it was a doll out called Busy Bee, Spelling Bee or something when she was little. Wendy, we used to just call her Wendy and JuJu was JuJu because they were all little.

We used to sing songs and make songs up about each other. We would really laugh at the songs we made up about each other. Then my little sister got up, she ran away and got pregnant twice, went through a whole bunch of hardship. She is doing real good now, but it was drama, it was drama ... And my little brother JuJu, he stayed there in the foster home, but they treated him kind of rough, told him he had a disease and he wasn't this or that.

I was told I couldn't see them, like when I used to come back and forth, I was told I was a pimp and would be a bad impression on my brothers and sisters. When we were living at home, I had to tie them up. The old man eventually had to do jail time. I'm out here working at night and they were running the streets. This is the drama that I had to go through. I come back and nobody would be in the house.

My little sister, Wendy could not be no more than about 11-12, somewhere like that and she was looking halfway decent, but in that environment we were living in, there were a bunch of perverts and freaks. Although she had already learned how to survive and knew what was happening by all the company the old man used to have coming through there and *ain't* no telling, and even some of our relatives would try to sleep with her. That's how scandalous it was, for all of us, even for the boys.

You weren't even safe around some of the men that wanted to be women. You know, you never like got violated. They had sex with you or took you out, now they might have asked to suck your dick and got to suck it, you might have fucked them or whatever have you, it was just that scandalous. But game is game. It was hard. And right now, you should be really messed up in the head. You shouldn't even know how to function. You should be just so crazy and pass this madness, this evil around to another set, to another generation. No, the buck stops here.

I'm not mad at the world, I'm not mad at those that did what they did. I'm not mad at the ones that lied on me, the ones that put me in jail. I'm not mad at them. I can't be. I have a life, and I'm going to constantly have a life. Even when this book comes out, I will have a life.

Everything I did, I did it because I had to. It was called survival, and I survived all this time. This is why the world is so messed up and they're telling you it's alright to be gay. They're telling you it is alright to like women, ladies to like ladies, men to like men, this is natural, and this is what they're telling you. There is nothing natural about that, ain't nothing natural about that. And then you know, you turn on the TV and they show you how to act when you feel like this towards another man or another woman. So it's got to be something wrong here.

I'm not mad at the world. All I'm asking you to do is read this book. Take something out of it that you can use and use it to better ourselves. Let's see if we can become a unit again. And like I was just saying, with all that happening, I turned out alright.

Nick-Nick stayed there in the foster home. He's somewhat all right; I hope he's all right too. You know, I always talk to him, just like I talk to my other brothers and sisters where we won't really let this drama bring us down and beat us down, because we know what's happening. We need to talk about it. We talk to each other about it, and we know that it had to happen and then you don't have all this pressure on you. That's how I made it, and some of them. They got tricked by the system and the streets also, but they had a choice in that situation. I say, I'm not going to just blame all this on the system and make it seem like the world done us so bad and things.

You do have a choice in the situation; that's what I did. I used to tell my brothers and sisters that. We have a choice. We could either be this, live this same life, or we could change. We have a choice. We can always be sitting here waiting for a check to come, we could be strung out, we could like alcohol, we could go out there and sell pussy, dope or whatever else you want to do, be a pimp; you could do whatever you want to do. Now you already saw this world and this is what you want to do, we can live this type of violence; you can do this. We can stay here, we can get stuck. We can act like these things are not happening. We can do this, or we can do better, and I'm constantly trying to do better.

You know in any minute, any second, I can turn my head and everything will be gone, this would be like a big dream or it could be like a nightmare--or it could be a nightmare. Like I always ask people, how can you be the doctor and end up the patient? It's like that because you thought you were better; you were pointing your finger.

Some people might like this book, while some might not. This is a chance I'm going to have to take. I have to be real about my childhood, and the experiences that got me to where I am today.

CHAPTER SIX

I would like to just say that after the kids had got through all of that, and I was going back and forth to visit my siblings -- now have you, after I graduated from Manley, they had put me in jail.

The principal named Blaine Deny at Manley had me put in jail, talking about I incited a riot, and all I did was broke it up. It would have been a riot, but I stopped that really quickly. Then uh, uh, when he found out that it wasn't my fault, I was released from jail.

I got put in jail about twice over at Manley for things that weren't my fault, but by the kids knowing me as being silly and outgoing and the hard life we lived, I was more of an example. The second time, I went to jail is because these boys were gon' jump on me; it was about eight of them. What I did, I didn't whip all eight of them. I would've been crazy as a bat trying to whip eight of these damn boys. I took out the first two. The two that were doing the most talking--I beat the shit out of them, and I took them to the office and put them on the principal's desk. I went to jail though. They told me I wasn't scared of them because I was supposed to be crazy in their eyes!

These brothers were trying to bring that gang banging stuff back. They said I was crazy; these brothers will tell you to this day, they're doing all right probably now too, but they will tell you, I didn't do anything to them. They just didn't like me and there's nothing I can do about that.

Even when I was in Hess, it was one boy that used to chase me, throw bricks at me and I could never catch this boy ... you understand. I would've *broke* him up, but I could never catch him. He would always have a whole bunch of boys with him that would chase me; and you know I *ain't* no fool either. Now I will run, okay. I will run; you know to save myself, because back then they hurt you just like they do nowadays, but they were more or less just didn't like you type deal and that's the way it went sometimes.

Now back to Manley ... after I got out of Manley, I was so glad to have graduated from school, but I still, at the same time, had needed to find myself again, because I'm still living in a mad type environment.

Dope man is still out there, my Father is getting high. I was going by, checking on him, making sure he was all right while I was still living with my Uncle. My Father felt I called DCFS on him. He called me a bitch, faggot, *hoe* and all this shit, but I still went and looked out for him, until he found out what happened because I didn't know anything about it till after I heard the kids were gone. I wasn't doing anything like that anyway. I just was trying to make sure I could do something to help him especially my family.

In the area that we lived, everybody was some kin to somebody. Everybody was having sex with each other, so you were almost somebody's cousin. This is the environment that we lived in, this neighbor would do it to them when they were drinking and getting high which was a no-win situation. This is just part of the situation that we would have to go through and deal with in that environment. Some of the guys, they wouldn't go to school because they didn't have to, it was the norm.

I tried to attend school at Malcolm X College but when I got to the college, I found out I wasn't able to handle it, so, I decided to go to Florida.

At that particular time, when I went to Florida, I was working for Dave County; when I first got there, keep in mind before that, I had a job as an Andy Frain Usher. As an Andy Frain Usher, this gave me the chance to get out of the neighborhood and ride the buses and go into different communities.

When I was an Andy Frain Usher, we did baseball games, football games, hockey, we did uh, wrestling, we did all the concerts; Barry White and whoever else came in. We did the Amphitheater, the Arie Crown Theater, we got to see plays, operas, and so on and so forth.... Then from there, I had got a job at the Tremont Hotel.

We were already around a lot of fancy cars and fancy clothes. Then when I started working for the Tremont Hotel, that gave me a chance to see nice, fancy, luxurious hotels, I was able to park different cars and ride in different cars; Rose Royce's, limousines, Jaguars; the valets got a chance to get inside them and drive around.

At the time, I was doing a lot of dancing; we were going to places called the Happy Medium, Dingbats, and the Underground. We were just partying because I was a party animal and was winning a few dance contests. I even used to dance where Mr. T used to be a bouncer. Everywhere Mr. T was a bouncer, I was always this hard, young guy, but I made my money. You may have got a regular check but you also had tips. I would always put my money up.

You have to expose yourself to a lot of different things, food, culture and different people; and that's what I did when I had all these different jobs, they introduced me to a wide range of people. This was different from what I was more familiar with.

This new bunch of kids that's coming up think they're gangsters and hard. We really lived hard. They just, now as far as being rappers and stuff, are just scratching the surface. If they really had to live it, you wouldn't say anything about it. In my opinion, you really wouldn't.

This is the same game, but it just has a different name. It's the same twist, the same dance, however, you want to call it, it's the same life ... all they did was add a little more money and put a little more higher stakes on your life. Your life is still worth nothing. If you are pushing it and giving it, you are killing the rest of us.

After that, I decided to go down to Florida. When I got to Florida, I worked in Miami Florida. When I got there, I got a job at a restaurant first being a busboy at an Italian restaurant and then I was staying in the YMCA. The YMCA is torn down now, but I was introduced to espresso and the different Cubans that were coming to Florida; there were black Cubans, and then you had some that came from the Islands also, and they would work for a little bit of nothing.

I worked for Dave County, wanted to use a crane and stuff like that, I did not get a chance. I wanted to use any claim, but I didn't get a chance to get a hold of none of that. I just hung out there for a while, just so I could get my head together. No one was there to help me, so I really had to make it on my own.

After being there for a while, it really wasn't going *nowhere*, I had to come back to Chicago. I applied for a job in Florida at a carpet place got hired, but I didn't start because it was time for me to go back to Chicago.

Once I got back to Chicago, I walked around for a while, got a job over there at the record shop; working for Batney's Records, and they really looked out for me and you know, I made me a little bit of money. Found time to go skating.

I went back to the Tremont Hotel, and got hooked up with a little white girl. It wasn't like we were going together, but she invited me out to go look at some clothes or something. Because I came back late messing around with her going shopping I was released from that job.

I joined the Army, and had a whole new experience. I also noticed the things that the black people did in the late 50's early 60's, now the Hispanic brothers and sisters are doing it. Like you saw a black woman, she had a lot of kids and she would run around with a lot of kids, and it would mostly be a single parent mom or the mom and the dad would be working, he would do the maintenance, janitor type job and will take care of the yard work and things like this. Now if you notice, all of the Hispanics are doing it.

When the black people act like they didn't understand what the white man was saying, they're kids were going to college. It's the same thing that's happening with the Hispanic people right now. Like they would give us the free shots, the flu shots, give us the sugar pills with the medicine on it. And we would have all our shots and they would have all these little different community things going on for us; same for the Hispanics right now.

Now they're stating that in about the year 2005, the Hispanics will be taking over; they will be the new Minority group in America. Where does that put us? That's saying we're obsolete? Our Hispanic brothers and sisters feel like they're going to beat the system, but if they know they're history way back when Morris conquered Spain, they sold us out to Christianity once before when they killed that Golden Goose. Again, history tends to repeat itself. A person ignoring their history is destined to repeat it.

When I joined the Army, I joined the army in Chicago. The army recruiting station was located on Madison Street. I passed the free test and I had passed the regular military test. I was placed in the Army and they told me not to take anything. So I gave everything I had to my brother David which was a lot of nice clothes and other nice things.

CHAPTER SEVEN

The first place the army sent me was Fort Dix, New Jersey, I had signed up to be an engineer that was a four year program. They sent me to Fort Dix, New Jersey for basic training. When I got to Fort Dix New Jersey, I went through the basic training.

I did everything they asked me, no problem. But they had a problem with me. I already had been working all my life at night. I had already been out on the street, so it was nothing but just to follow directions, which I did very well. The problem came when they wanted to curse me out, call me all kinds of names, and I explained to them, I could have stayed out on the streets for all this.

I also had problems with going ahead and completing my task. I completed them but it still wasn't good enough. They would put me through a lot. We would go for long walks, no problem; that didn't bother me. The exercise, no problem, that didn't bother me. I was eating a lot of fruits and vegetables and that didn't bother me. They would run people to death, that didn't bother me. Clean up, that didn't bother me. Didn't anything bother me, and they were getting kind of pissed off because I'm like that now. Like I said before earlier, ask me if I give a fuck. It didn't bother me.

They really want to know, who is this guy? Let's start checking; so they sent me through the gas chamber, I come out, I'm alright. They sent me through there three more times. The other guys went through there once, but they came out coughing. They already told us what to do before we went into the gas chambers. In the community I grew up in we were getting gassed down, so you know, it wasn't anything to me; smelling something and holding my breath.

I already know how to swim; and when we jump off the little cliffs and things, I already knew how to swim, so the brothers are like, where did this brother come from?

The drill sergeant called me in there. By this time they were treating me really bad, I was doing everything they were saying; I was passing. They were telling me that I wasn't gone graduate, and then they told me that I should get out of the army, and I told them no, I'll sign up for a career or something, so I passed the next test, but they wouldn't let me out till a few weeks after the others.

I graduated then they sent me out to Fort Leonard Wood, MS. That was called the "Million Dollar Hole." In the million dollar hole, you learn about cranes, forklift, drive line, bucket loaders, dump trucks, and things of this nature. After we put on all these little different things, it was more or less a power struggle, they told me that I was a problem and that I could make people do things I wanted them to do. They sent this from Fort Dix, New Jersey. Now they already made me low crawl, I can smell New Jersey all over my face Jack. They made me low crawl all through New Jersey; Jumping Jacks running around with guns over my head, yelling, "This is my rifle, this is my gun, this is for killing, this is for fun." They really just made me out of a problem because I just wasn't gone just take you abusing me. I have taken enough abuse as it is.

I would complete that task. It wasn't like I was doing anything, like hitting them or nothing or going off, but I was telling them, they were going to have to do a little bit better than this. I came here for a trade, all he had to do was do his job; let me go ahead and do what I had to do and go about my business somewhere. So, they sent a bad report with me, stating that I'm a bad little guy.

When I get to Fort Leonard Wood, MS, I already had an X on my back. Then when I get there, I'm doing my job, taking care of my business and stuff like this and was treated worse than when I was in Fort Dix, New Jersey.

In the military I was taught how to operate equipment, use tool bands, bucket loaders, drag mines, graters, bulldozers, dump trucks and so on and so forth. It was so much to learn. No matter how difficult it became, I dealt with it and functioned under pressure. Being in the military was nothing compared to living in a war zone—the environment I grew up in. I wanted to do a career. I get up in there and they start messing with me again.

The boys that were in the military were getting high. They would do their little thing and everybody would get high. Getting high was not my interest. I didn't have to get high-been there, done that, saw that movie.

When I first got high, when I first got my first joint, I was about seven years old. My Uncle introduced us to some reefer, my Uncle Billy, gave us a couple hits. See reefer always has been around. You see they used to smoke it when they used to do their singing and shit like that, so you know, and I been smoking cigarettes ever since I was eleven years old. I'm 20-21, maybe 22, somewhere up in that area, I didn't need to get high. I hadn't been getting high all this time.

When I got high, it made me paranoid, it made me very paranoid and I didn't like that. I like to know what I am doing at all times. Reefer made me feel as if I didn't. I don't like that at all. There you have it. I didn't like getting high at all.

My time in the Military: I left from Chicago and was stationed in Fort Dix, New Jersey. My M.O.S. was 62 Fox Trot, Engineer. When I got to New Jersey, It was all right; I went through my basic training, I did everything that was demanded of me.

I had problems with a couple of drill sergeants that pulled me in the office one day when I was sitting down there and they told me I need to quit--I need to get out of the service; and I refused.

They put the chairs on my ankle while I was sitting down there, they said, "you gonin' quit; you gonin' quit." And they already were getting high as well, and I'm stating again, I'm not saying anything bad about the Military. I just wanted to do a career; the Military was all right for me.

The Military was very good. The only reason I joined the Military is because I knew, I would not be able to go to school or to continue my education or have different options; like jobs, or be able to buy a house, or have some kind of medical benefits, if I did not join the Military.

I had a girlfriend, whose mother told me I was too serious; because I was telling her daughter what I wanted to do. I was thinking about going into Mortuary Science, but that blew over real fast because I didn't have any money to go; and I wasn't prepared educationally for this because we had to have Biology and Science courses.

We learned how to seek out mines; I learned how to detonate a mine, and how to discharge a mine. If you were to step on it, they would send us in. We also learned how to place plastic explosives in different areas. I was going through that and I started this in A.I.T. (Advance Intense Training) and then I was sent to permanent party. This is where you finish off the rest of your military time.

During the evening hours, I would do a little boxing, you know, on the heavy bag and speed bag, to keep a lot of these frustrations off of me. I was boxing for them. I was whipping everything coming my way tearing them up. I fought until all this anger came out of me. You see, I wasn't angry at the world anymore, so I quit boxing. Then I started working out.

There was a white guy that would come in there who was famous who I will leave nameless. He would be able to go out and get drunk; drive around, all the rest of us had to stay inside the barracks. I don't know who this man was *Reverend House Cat*. He kept us in trouble. One day we were sitting down doing our work and he hollered at me and called me a Nigga, so I didn't say *nothing* at first, so he just kept on provoking me, so I just leaned back and kicked him in the face with my boot. I just kicked his ass straight off the damn couch! And then he said, "I thought you were a smart ass Nigga, I thought you was one of the smartest Niggas we had." I didn't know who this man was, so after that I really started having problems with some more people.

They let me stay. After we finished A.I.T., I finished; I completed all the terms with them, but they made me stay behind and let the other ones go on over to their permanent party. I got out of A.I.T., a little later than everybody else.

While I was waiting to complete my time, this time they had me cleaning out the parking lots, painting the officer's office. They just sent me through a whole bunch of changes, but I was able to get through that. I got through that because I still refused to quit.

They finally let me go and sent me to Fort Riley, Kansas; next to Leavenworth Prison. I guess they just knew I was going to prison; this is the idea I had when they sent me there. They're going to make sure you do something wrong. We already knew about dope and *hoes*, so they had a lot of Koreans that came over. They had lots of different stores. The Korean ladies were telling me what they would do for me.

They kept saying, "I just want to make you happy for one night." They continued, "You think I'm a *hoe*, I'm not no *hoe*." They were still out there selling sex in Kansas. I was taught earlier; I watched a lot of brothers; the dope dealers, the slick boys, the pimps, all of them who were doing so well, but still was buying sex. They were buying sex; they were tricks; they were their own best customers.

I grew up around a bunch of ladies who showed me some of the things they liked and what they didn't like. It would be at least one *hoe* that just drove the men crazy. The men would just let them do whatever they wanted to do to them. But this man, he was supposed to have been so hard and so cleaver, but he was a trick. He was the biggest trick. Most of the time when you're in this game, a lot of them become the trick baby. They were young tricks, grow up with old tricks. If you got the drugs and things like that, you would pay to take care of this broad's habit although you knew she was taking you for a ride.

To make a long story short, when I was in Fort Riley, Kansas, this is the permanent party you just had to do your eight hours. When I was in Fort Riley, Kansas, I started reading books and other reading material, I was still dancing. We would go to the Iron Horse. They used to call me "Cowboy" and "Chi-town". I was sharp and dress to kill. I used to wear cowboy boots, nice 40 gallon hats. The hats were called Stetsons. They were sharp; they were sharp, okay.

See I like to dress. They would check me out scanning me from my head to toe. Just like I shave my head bald now, I shaved it back then. They told me I didn't have to keep it cut like that, but I used to keep mine cut short anyway, and they would think I was just a trainee, so I would get sent through a whole bunch of changes.

I started going to the Library. The first book I took out at the library was called, "All The President's Men" by Carl Bernstein and Bob Woodward. This was dealing with Watergate. You have to sign these books out, so I took out a few books, and I don't know what the other few books were, but I signed them out.

When I came back to the library, I was met by an officer who called me in and told me to come here, he showed me his identification and he was asking me about the book. "Why did I take this book out, and asked if can I read this book?" He told me to read it to him. When I was ah, I told him I didn't want to read it out loud because I have a hard time with the words. I said, "I can read it to myself and tell you what this paragraph is saying, and whatever page you pick out I can read it and tell you exactly what it says." He said all right, so I read it, and I explained to him what it was; he turned red and after that he left and then I went back to my unit. I kept checking books out of the library because by this time I had learned how to start completing books. You start it from the beginning, and go to the end.

Because I quit boxing, they gave me so much trouble. They wanted me to fight for them and I refused because my focus was on being a leader. I asked if I could go to the Officer Candidate School, but they refused to let me go even though they would say that I have leadership skills. No matter what I did, it still wasn't enough.

Their tactic of control was brainwashing so that I would get frustrated and start back boxing for them. If I don't let you sleep, and I'm constantly hollering at you-screaming at you, got you running, exercising, you just start doing things automatically. That's the same way with these different cults and everything else that you would get involved in.

When you pledge, those that have been to college, they keep you so busy, that you just automatically do things; just be on a zone which is just a form of brainwashing. If you're not shown any affection, you know, hugging and talking kind to you, but hollering at you and making you do more exercise, it is a tactic to make you do what they want you to do.

When you go to these religious types of organizations, they hug you, show you kindness, keep you up, having you constantly doing things, and only eating certain kinds of food, drinking certain kinds of water, they have changed your diet, by doing this, they have changed your mind. Same way with the Military, it's nothing but a bigger form of brainwashing.

Although I did what they wanted me to do, they still put me in bad boy's camp, and told me to do pushups to sergeant rock and other difficult tasks. Sergeant rock is actually a rock not a person. While doing pushups, I had to say out loud, one sergeant rock, two sergeant rocks, and so on and so forth.

What really got me in trouble, I would tell them certain things that they would do was wrong, like when they would grab me in my collar. I would say, "You don't have to put your hands on me. Don't put your hands on me; this is not what I suppose to do. Your job is to give me an order, for me to do it, you can holler and do whatever you want to do; curse, and do whatever, but I *ain't* come here for that; I came here to learn a trade." This is what would get me in trouble because you know all that is--ah, what really made them mad, they didn't intimidate me.

See I had that look, like I say, I got the mask, I got the look, I got the street look, I'm just a hard looking guy sometimes; if I'm not smiling. You don't want to be around me when I'm not smiling. They found that out and when they see that they can't intimidate you with all these threats and with all this punishment, they do everything else to do things to you.

They had to send me to bad boy's camp, and I did exactly what they wanted done. Although, it was somewhat difficult, we were put out in the field, cutting grass when the sergeant left. Twelve lawn mowers out on the field and the sergeant making us go around in a circle and told us he wanted every area cut. What I did, I broke everybody down and put one boy over each area: one in this area, one in another area, and one boy over here. We all made these squares, into circles and it made this big circle.

The entire lawn was cut when he came back. We had that done about an hour. In an hour, we were sitting down waiting for him to come back. And he got mad, "Who in the hell told y'all to cut this grass like that; who cut this grass?" It was looking good; it was looking great. It wasn't looking bad, it was looking really manicured. He couldn't say anything but that the project was supposed to last for almost two weeks, so there was nothing left for us to do. Now, they got to find something else. Once again, they were mad at me again.

After I got out of there, I got out because the Lieutenant asked them, "What is this man in here for?" You know, he did so and so. I told them, "Officer, I *ain't* done *nothing*." He said, "That man *ain't* crying because y'all hurting him, that man crying because he can't do nothing to y'all, and he knows he hasn't done anything."

I used to always tell them, now you know I haven't done nothing, what is all this about? What it was, they wanted me to quit and get out of the Military; they wanted me to get out of there before my time and with a dishonorable discharge. I hadn't done anything to be dishonorable. I was *being* nothing but a soldier. Sent back to my unit, I continued to do what I did.

I would go to the library and do some more reading and when we got our holiday time-off: I would leave and *shoot* up here to Chicago, because it was close to us the same way when I used to do in Fort Leonard Wood, Missouri.

Chicago is close to Kansas, Missouri, so I would shoot back up to Chicago and see how my brothers were doing. I sit *in* the back of the bus with my camouflage on looking different from everyone else. I would just show up creeping and surprise them. Being around them kept me abreast to the street. When I get back to Chicago from the Military, I am going to have to come back to it, so I do not want to lose my street sense. Because when I got out and returned, they would've tore me up, so you had to keep that balance of where you come from; even now.

For instance, if you go into a higher learning institution, or whatever you're doing, never forget where you came from, never forget the game. Like I told you before, game recognizes game. It's the same game, different flavor. It's the same game, different time.

Even from back in the Pyramid days, they had game back then, if you look on the Pyramid walls, just like what's written in the Bible, the Holy Qur'an, the Jewish Torah and anything else, these are written on the walls of the Pyramids, that came before the Bible and before the birth of Jesus and so on and so forth.... Just like they had the birth of Jesus, you had the birth of Isis and Osiris.

* * *

I'm just throwing little things in here for you all to understand. Take what I am saying literally and refer to a book of reference or do your own research. This is what I'm trying to show you throughout the pages of this book. I made it through all the adversity, and I am giving you examples of how I made it.

Okay to keep on going on ... now that I have been going back and forth from Chicago not bothering anybody doing what I was supposed to do, all of a sudden the sergeants at the motor pool, started taking away my position using cranes. They had brought me in and told me they wanted me to drive the Jeep for the lieutenant. The reason why I do not want to drive the Jeep is because you can get crushed by the tanks and heavy motor equipment. This was not my MOS. When I started, I was positioned to be a Heavy Equipment Operator Engineer.

I had heard earlier that, some dude had got hurt in one of the jeeps. They want me to drive the jeep even when the lieutenant is not there. Even when the lieutenant is not in the Jeep, they would want me to run errands. I could get killed maneuvering in between the tanks. I believe this was their intentions on getting rid of me.

I did not join the military to become a tank driver nor a Jeep driver. I was trained in Fort Leonard Wood, Missouri to be a crane operator. I drop the bucket loader, while on a crane down into the ground, open it up and grab the dirt then lift it to a pile on the surface of the ground and continue until I receive word that the task is completed.

In addition, here is another example of how they are trying to bring me harm. There was a soldier on the crane operating it. The back part of the crane titled as if it was going to fall forward because of the weight of the bucket loader. At that point, the soldier was instructed to move the crane closer to the edge then I was instructed to get on it. I refused. I was furious to a point of anger but couldn't show what was going on inside my mind. All I could say, is, "I am not getting on that crane. I I I be damned if I'm gone sit there....

'Now, I wasn't born here just yesterday either. You know, you see danger, you know danger when you see it; and that was danger. And I wasn't about to climb up in there trying to mess around with that big old crane and all that wire and going down in that hole and it's tipping over like that, then I'll be crushed.'"

I'll tell you what he didn't do; he did not get in that crane either. Once the crane was moved back a little bit, I completed the task. Soldiers were standing in formation when one after another started repeating, "You do it." Another would say, "No. You do it. You climb up in there." One began to explain, "If you go in the crane and climb up in there, if you let that thing go down very fast, it just might tip right over."

I said, "You just showed us what these cranes can do, how to surf the cable, what the drums are, we just got finished learning all about every part on this thing and what it was capable of doing. How do you expect me to climb up there knowing that it might tip over? No way Jose! You climb up in there!"

What the sergeant did to intimidate me, yelling and getting in my face didn't mean *nothing* to me. That didn't mean anything to me. If you think back to when I mentioned earlier about the old man putting shotguns in my face, making me hold pistols, constantly in front of my face saying; you no good, stupid son-of-a-bitch. This was worse than the drill sergeant. That military wasn't shit compared to my real life. It wasn't *nothing*. After that, they sent me to bad boy school—you know, I graduated, I finished.

After that, they sent me to my permanent party, the "Big Red One" Fort Riley, Kansas. They put me next to Leavenworth prison. They put me through all of this. Now they are thinking *he's gone blow up any minute now he's gonna snap.* Since I already knew what they were doing, I thought to myself *No I'm not. I wasn't gonna snap. I'm not no fool, like I told you, I'm not crazy.* I know y'all setting me up and y'all have rules and regulations-for black people. There are two different sets of rules: it's called conditional and unconditional. When it comes to them, it's conditional when it comes to us it's unconditional--flat line.

After we finished formation, we went to the motor pool every morning to fulfill our duties. I had six pairs of boots, 12 working uniforms that were just green, that wasn't camouflage; it was just solid green Khaki, and a little cap which was my work uniform. I had 12 of them. I was dressed-right-dress. When I got dirty in the motor pool in the morning, before I went to eat lunch, I went and changed my uniform.

One particular day I came down to formation; I was dressed-right-dress; they asked me why I keep cutting my hair. I told them because it looked good to me. Every time they saw me, I was dressed-right-dress. When I went to eat lunch, for formation, and everywhere I went on post, I was dressed-right-dress. Then one sergeant told me I'm making him look bad.

While in Fort Riley, Kansas, the sergeants would ask us, "Soldier, where are you from?" We would say, "Big Red One." Then we were so proud of our M.O.S. that we would say, "Engineer, Sir." Even while we were in formation, I would call cadence.

> "I know a girl that lives on a hill. She won't do it, but her sister will. Sound off, one two; sound off, three four, sound off one two, three four."

CHAPTER EIGHT

After all of this, they were still trying to make me box for them. I mentioned earlier that I wanted to stop boxing, but they thought it would be best for me to continue. Since I did not want to box any longer, they took away my privileges and put me in bad soldier camp. I couldn't go off post; I had to stay in the barracks. It was very difficult just going to eat and only going to certain places. I had to be close by whenever they called for me. I had to be wherever they wanted me to be. This is another form of stopping me from moving around or even mingling with the other people there.

Then I found out there were people from my neighborhood in Chicago that were in the military. Some of them were even dope fiends that used to shoot dope at my old man's house. One of them was even my girlfriend's brother, he was in there. It's a small world, but they didn't want me to mingle with anyone. They already had the idea that I could make them start a riot when I wanted to. This thing has been following me ever since I left Manley high school.

They already know your history, so they went and found something. All through history they tend to always make us out of rebels, or anti-, semi's-, anything they can name, they come up with some European word to make it seem like you're really, bad. We all should be almost tired of this by now. This game has been played, I told you earlier, about the infinite *Willie Lynch Letter*, "Don't trust nobody but me." Then they know how to work this system- this *vein*. They teach their kids this way of viewing us.

After I go through all these changes and did what I was supposed to do, they couldn't find anything wrong with that. I was able to complete that bad soldier camp.

Sergeant Jones was one of the key players in holding me back. He wanted to be promoted in the Fire Department on post. He was a career soldier who could not make it in the real world which we called lifers. A lifer is someone who makes a career out of being in the military. They are career soldiers. If they went out into the real world, they could not make it.

The real world is a horse of a different color. That's why they had to stay in there so long. See, it didn't bother me to go in the real world, like I told them I can make it in the real world. I would tell them, that they would get torn up in the real world. They didn't like that even though I was telling the truth. They were more or less used to a controlled environment just like colleges, universities, higher learning institutions, and prison systems. All of these are controlled environment structures through our government. It's nothing like the real world.

Because of what I was saying, they admitted me to a crazy hospital. I mean literally crazy hospital. This is where they gave me this gown to put on backwards. The only thing outside of the gown that I had on was my underwear. They put me through a series of tests: by starting with my name to asking me if I heard conversations while they were asking me questions. The questions that were asked was psychological questions to see how balanced I was.

In this crazy hospital there were soldiers pretending to be crazy so that they could get a medical discharge. While I was in there, I would ask some how is it that you can't walk now but you were walking before you got in the service; you were in your right mind, and now you aren't; now you have been diagnose as crazy taking Thorazine to which the doctors wanted to prescribe to me stating that I was too hyper. I kept convincing them that there was nothing wrong with me. I would be very careful about what I was eating and drinking.

They would break me down by making me hold sand bags over my head while it was raining, drilling me to say, "This is my riffle, this is my gun. This is for killing and this is for fun." The weight and the strain of this procedure hurt my back, swelled my lips and my face. I still didn't give up you know they wouldn't let me go to the doctor. This was a case of a mistaken identity.

An Uncle of mine name Leroy Davis was also in the Military. When he was given Thorazine, he lost his mind. I knew that there wasn't anything wrong with me. They wanted me to take this medicine even after I saw how others were reacting from taking it. I always have been careful about who I am. I am always in my right mind no matter what they were saying. Wasn't *nothing* wrong with me. I am very careful about what I eat and what I drink, especially while I was in the military. I have always been like that.

My Uncle Leroy Davis lost his mind. From what I understand, he was bright before he went in there. I remember him even playing with us when we were children. He seemed like he was a cool dude, you know. One day while in Chicago, all of a sudden, the next time I see him he was down here in the crazy hospital walking around acting crazy as a *Betsy bug*. I wasn't going out like that.

I associated everything that I account for in my life, I learn twenty four-twenty four. I don't even sleep that much because I think I'm gone miss something.

During this time, they sent me through all these changes and they told me I should take the Thorazine, and they even offered me a military discharge. It was a whole bunch of them in that war that was trying to get a military discharge because they had broken them down.

First, I explained to them if we take this Thorazine and this medicine that they want to administer and you keep taking it if you do not need it, it can make you crazy. If we passed the exam that proved we were mentally stable, then we were alright when we joined.

Secondly, what kind of job would we get if we were considered as a disabled vet? Mentally disabled? We would be considered as crazy. Who's going to hire a crazy person? No body. So, no I refuse to take the medicine and be labeled as a military discharge-medical.

I would get up every day, do my jumping jacks; my sit ups, my exercise, like I still do now till this day. I also like to dance, so I would be dancing and doing whatever I got to do; a little shadow boxing, just to keep my mind fresh.

When I get up in the morning, they were sitting around looking at cartoons and *thangs* ... acting goofy, and wanting to put their head in the water. There was one guy that wouldn't get out the bed. There was another guy telling me I should take this military discharge. He believed that he was going to be a preacher. During this time, I was studying the Bible. This is not my first time reading the Bible.

The military gave us little green bibles that were really, really small. I used to carry it around with me and look through it, although I had to squint my eyes in order to read it. I also had small magazines to read.

When I get up and turn the television to Good Morning America, the doctors used to get mad. They wanted· to put it back on the cartoons. They would take a vote and ask everyone, "Who all want to look at Good Morning America raise they hands?" We all raised our hands. A lot of them who they had labeled crazy got well even the one who wouldn't get out of bed. I took some popcorn in the room and was eating it then I asked him did he want some. He said, "Yeah." I told him he had to get up and get it. I say, they want you to think you're crazy man; they want you lying over there. So, the young man got up and started coming out.

Noticing that I was helping those in the military hospital, they hurried up and got me out of there. I was no longer marked as crazy after everybody started acting· normal around there.

The medical staff came to me and told me I was not the doctor. Their exact words are, "You are not the doctor here Mr. Davis." I say, "I *ain't* trying to be the doctor. I just want them to get up and let them know *ain't* nothing wrong with them."

The following day, I had been there for a while. I went in and I asked them, "Do you want me to act crazy? Do you want me to throw this TV down on the ground and put my head through it? Is this what you want me to do to get up out of here? What do I have to do to get up out of here? There's nothing wrong with me. I've been going along with the program. You are wrong to put me in here anyway. I didn't just walk up in here, you decided to put me in here, and you know it *ain't nothing* wrong with me."

I wouldn't drink their Kool-Aid®. I wouldn't just let them give me anything. Even when I used to go eat, I refused to eat food that was sitting there waiting for me. No. I watched them make my food; you don't just give me *nothing*. I had already been doing the vegetarian thing.

While I was there, I ate bananas and toast. See, because when you put something in the banana, you got to abuse that banana, that banana will have a bruise mark on it. I ate toast with no butter just some bananas and dry toast. I'll drink water that I got for myself. I would not let them give me anything to put me to sleep at night.

Finally, after that, they decided to let me go. When they sent me back to the unit, they were scared to death. They told me, "Mr. Davis, you got to stay in your room, you can't be walking around." I said, "No problem." You know, I was cool. I listened to music knowing that it was a setup. I just had to wait it out to see what the setup was going to be.

Sergeant Jones told me to go back to the barracks. His exact words were, "Mr. Davis, go back to the barracks. Your work is done, go on. We know where to find you." They kept coming to see what being in the barracks having nothing to do was doing to me.

All of sudden the game they were playing was exposed. About two or three weeks later, they say, "We have been looking for you." I say, Sergeant Jones told me I can go back to my barracks." Then Sergeant Jones said, "No, I *ain't* tell you nothing like that."

See, they set me up. They killed me with a pencil and a piece of paper. They made it seem as if I was not following orders. They know if I was supposed to be at the motor pool, and I was supposed to have been there, my work would have been completed.

I loved what I did: inspecting the tools, preparing the paperwork to submit of broken or cracked equipment. It was not a difficult job. I always had my vans, dressed-right-dress. I kept my motor pool area neat for whenever they had to rent a tool.

I've been living hard all my life. In the military, I was given a room, shelter and food. I didn't have to pay rent, so I decided to put my money up. This way I could pay for my education. I put away some bonds. Man I was in heaven! I wasn't gone never come out of there if I didn't have to. They made me come out.

After all this, they called me in and they sent me over to an In-house Court Martial. It turned out all the way different. What it was, they called me down there and they had the in-house court martial there saying what I did, so I went to the Full Bird Colonel's house and said, "Hey man, I *ain't* doing nothing to these people and they constantly sending me through all these changes; and I even had everybody in our barracks to sign this thing stating that I haven't done anything to be treated like this or saying that I'm doing all this different stuff. All I'm doing is functioning."

During the time, I went to the Colonels house and asked can I speak to him. I told those in the office who I was and where I was stationed, but I didn't get a chance to see the officer, of course, because you have to go through the chain of commands. When that got back, they were upset; because I needed to approach it differently.

The way we grew up, we weren't talking about lawyers, attorneys, and things like this. We didn't have any idea of all this kind of stuff. So, they gave me an in-house hearing. What they did, they told me that it was a couple of them that knew me. Some of them I used to box for. Because I was not in the click, I did not have their support.

When you are in the military just like out here in the police force, and anywhere else, they all have to stay together. If it's a lie, we all got to keep our lie together. Everybody better say the same thing. One of them told me, I wasn't a soldier. I presented the papers and everything, saying that I hadn't done this, and I didn't do this and you know, I call myself doing what I am supposed to do. They gave me one of them little old guys that supposed to be there, that supposed to be on my side, but he was with them also. I told them that I haven't done anything.

Sergeant Jones was there and all the others. They had it hooked up; they denied all of it. As I said earlier, they killed me with a pencil and a piece of paper. Even though the military papers from the medical place showed that there wasn't anything wrong with me, they really had to get rid of me.

They asked me, why did I come here? I told them, I came here for a career. This is when they told me that I can incite riot. These people would do anything I tell them to do; they could tear this post down. I asked them; because we were in the meeting, why don't you send me to Officer Candidate School? If I'm all this much of a threat, and I got all this leadership potential, send me to Officer Candidate School. I encouraged them that this is what you need, you need leaders, send me to Officer Candidate School, and then they said, "Well no, no."

I said, "You know there wasn't anything wrong with me; you sent me through all these changes all these years and I made it." I told them, "All I wanted to do was a career here. All I wanted to do was go to school, pay for my house, when I get finished. I wanted to have my military benefits; this is what I wanted; this is why I joined here so I can have somewhere to go. I can be able to do something better with my life; this is the reason why I joined. They asked, "Is that the reason why you're here

Mr. Davis?" I answered, "Yeah, that's why I'm here." Not realizing that they were going to go back and have a brief discussion amongst themselves.

At that point, I was dismissed. When they brought me back in the room after they dismissed me, they brought me in and told me just like this, you have an honorable discharge. Hence, you have a military discharge up under honorable conditions. You will receive all your veteran's benefits; you are a vet. You've been here long enough to be a vet. Because you know, you had to be a year and some months to become a vet at that particular time. They gave me everything that I wanted, but I was so devastated that they really just let me go. Now I had to adjust very quickly. I had already been going back and forth to the city, so it wasn't like I was lost trying to figure out what was going on, on the street.

They gave me all my papers. I still had to let them know my observations of it all. I explained to them, I can see why this is all messed up now and how come the military is messed up, and why some black people have to do what they have to do. You think King, -X-, is bad, all you are doing is creating a monster here. I say that's all you're doing; you're creating a monster.

I left out of there with my discharge papers. I tried to get back in a couple of times, but they would not allow me access. There was nothing going on, on the street. It was slow motion. So, I came and I stayed with my sister.

CHAPTER NINE

When I get to my sister's house, she already got two little children and *thangs*, she was glad to see me at first, but she had a lil' pimp boyfriend there. This boy was *pimping* her. It was a nice place, but she had two babies. He was looking better than my sister. I was like, oh no, this motherfucker *ain't* no real pimp. I'm gone show him what a pimp is.

One day my sister was out there trying to get her money on, and I told her, "Baby, these your pimps right here, these two little motherfucking babies. If you gone go out there and make some money, you supposed to be making some money for them, you understand?"

I carried my pistol on me. It didn't bother me none, but this is the way we grew up, you know. And, hey, I didn't care. When she went out that night, I told her boy just like this; I said, "You know what, whatever she brings in, you got to double it." He asked, "What in the fuck are you talking about?" This is what he tells me. I said, "You heard me, I didn't stutter my brother. I continued, 'She is out there making money, out there selling pussy and shit.

Whatever she brings in, you better double it. You think I'm bullshitting? Okay, try me and don't do it, shit....'"

She went out there and got some money, I didn't know how much she brought in, but I just imagined how much she could've made. I told him I wanted a Grand from him. He said, "Who in the fuck you talking to?" I say, "You bitch!" Then I put the pistol in his face, I continued, "I told you I want a Grand, motherfucker, I'm gone show you a pimp. A pimp supposed to make the same amount of money or more than his *Hoe*; now get *yo* ass out there and make me some money!"

After that, that motherfucker thought I was crazy- that motherfucker thought I was crazy, okay? I was showing him, he wasn't *no* pimp; you understand what I'm saying, you ain't no pimp! Pimp pimp them all; pimp pimp lady, pimp pimp man, pimp pimp anything. You want to be a pimp, be a real pimp, bitch! You understand? That motherfucker, after that, left.

Wendy snapped on me, you understand.... She asked me, "What the fuck did you do?" I must say, my sister snapped on me. She asked me, what did I do with her man. Her ·man got the fuck out of there, that's what the fuck he did. She went out to look for him. He had her on some of that shit. She was losing it, she was losing it man ... and I saw it. She threw me in jail. I didn't have anywhere to go. I had to put my pistol up, because it was legal.

When I came out, I went on about my business and you know, then I went to my other sister's house and she had some Nigga there, all he wanted to do was drink; you understand. My little niece just lying there, so I took her, told her about the library and he got mad because I asked her, how in the fuck you gone bring home a drink and the baby running around here with paper on the floor? You're paper training her like a dog. Where is that motherfucker?

This is another sister. I get my ass thrown out of there. They put me in jail again.

I decide to go back to Kansas to try to see if I can get a job. Wasn't nothing happening; it was slow motion. I went back to the post, you know, looked around and some of the guys were there and I explained to them what was happening.

By this time, I am getting frustrated because they really just jerked me around, and I couldn't get *nothing* flying, I couldn't get nothing started. I couldn't get a decent job. So I bump around for a little while, because I had a little more money. I would bump around and do what I had to do.

After going back and forth to jail and then going up to Kansas, and thangs like that, I saw Sergeant Rink and whoever else I could, and explained it to them what I was doing and what I was trying to do, so I came on back here and did what I had to do.

My brother, name David, had his little girlfriend. I asked him about some clothes, and he asked, "You want all of it back?" I left that alone too. I then was hired at Bailey's Records as a delivery man. I stayed there for a while, until I just got tired.

I was with Aunt Bea, and she was treating me kind of weird as if I was doing something to her. During this time, I had started going back to Malcolm X too. I went back and forth, but I couldn't stay, because I really never had anywhere to stay even when I was with my sisters. I received my degree by finishing out a semester, leaving, and returning over a period of time until I finished.

Then I jumped up and went to California because I was here with the family, and nobody could help me or reach for me. I went to California, but I started off in San Francisco. I rode the bus down there in Fresco. I had to stay with some gay boys. I didn't have to have sex with them because I explained to them my situation and how they should be able to respect my background; that I'm not mad at them, you know, they can do what they do. Since I had already been around this type of environment, I've seen it already. That's your world. I was able to adjust.

I started working for Patty Hearst father's newspaper company as a security guard. I stayed there for about a month or so, two months to be exact. After work, I used to party at Euro 2000, down there near the Fisherman's Wharf on the Lake front. Some of the guys look just like ladies, you see what I'm saying, but my mind was just on dancing. I just wanted to dance.

We would dance to the song titled, "Funky Town." Then when it got tired, I really didn't like the environment, because that was not my lifestyle. It was an evil town to me. You could really sense how evil it was. From there I went to California; walked around on Sunset Strip. Since I always liked to skate and dance, I had my skates with me, so I went to this place called Flippers to skate.

I met this guy name Jay who said he was a manager. He said we'll go to Hollywood and be a skater, you understand. We'll make a skating movie. Somebody might see me and know my talent, I'm out there doing you know, a lil' bit of this, and a lil' bit of that. Then when I got out there, it was a lot of people there hanging out on the streets.

I had money from my veteran checks that was being mailed to my address. The checks would never come on time, so sometime they would pile up. My money was still going to my old address. While I'm in California, just hanging out, I had a lil' money from where I worked at the newspaper store. I was going to really try to make it, but it had got so bad and so ugly that a lot of them were strung out. It was some wild parties down on Sunset Strip. They would just be out on the street.

Because I had nowhere to go, I slept outside on some buses with no place to go. I watched some of the people take their dogs in the restaurant, and wouldn't help those who lived on the street. Even while I was in Chicago, I slept inside the warehouse they used to store big train engines on Sacramento. It has been torn down. I was blessed so many times, that I never got caught.

I used to sleep in abandoned buildings. And then some empty cars, you know during that period, I found out later, it was about pride. You didn't want anybody to know that you were all down and out. It was about pride. And then I found out, pride *ain't* shit! Pride will get you fucked up! Pride will make you starve to death. I found out, when I was going through that it's easy to give up. It's easier to give up and just do nothing. It's easier.

Do you know what the hardest part is? The hardest part is doing what I'm doing now, surviving, and continuing, setting goals, reaching for goals, achieving those goals to the best of my abilities and once you do that, you move on to another one. You must constantly, and I hope you all hear me very well when I tell you this, you must constantly, constantly, set goals for yourself. When you reach that goal, go on to another one. Start off setting goals that are not so high. This way you can reach them. It can be somewhat discouraging if you set a goal and you can't reach it, get you a reachable goal. For this reason, you can make it a little tiny goal at first. They get bigger and bigger every time. Just like I'm writing this book now, this is another goal.

I'm telling you about my life, but I'm also putting in a little information that you can use. If you do not have an economic background, read books on economics. You should do things like this, you know, the book is out there. I heard before, if you don't want a black person to know something, put it in a book. Read and you'll find out why you're here, and it *ain't* about they don't like you because you're black.

Think about it if they have sex with you, my brothers and sisters it takes them generations and generations to bring themselves to that natural blood. That's what this is all about, that's why they had to hang you. That's why they told you, you can't look at white women. You shouldn't want to look at them too tough no way, not as far as taking them home. See, you can get white from black, but you can't get black from white or from any other race. Once we mix with that race, they become us. And that's why they do not want you to pick up books to start reading them.

Pick up some books. Pick up some books, you'll find out what the real story is. Look in the dictionary. I'm not a genius, I'm still not. I, till this day, still have a hard time doing certain things. I struggle in many different areas, but I am not going to let anything hold me back. You shouldn't either. I still have problems with my spelling, pronunciation of some words, but I would take the time to understand it because most of us, we already have this insight of where if you show us, we will learn it. We will learn it better.

The people who taught everybody, how all of a sudden we know nothing? We are the first man. I always tell everybody, we need to quit feeling sorry for ourselves and just go ahead and do it, just try your best in everything you do.

How I was living out in the streets and how easy it is to become homeless and push the cart around, and get strung out, and do different little things. It's not that it's you, it's a set program. It's a set program. Now have you, I was telling you how I was coming all the way through this, and now all of a sudden, I was getting close to graduating out of Malcolm X college. During the time, I was graduating out of Malcolm X college it was more or less a time of confusion. Everywhere I went every house I stayed in, when it was time for me to graduate, it got worse and worse.

One day I purchased tickets to the Gap Band and the Isley Brothers' concert, they were at the Chicago Stadium. I was walking across the street, and the police just pointed me out of the *blue*. Wearing a military raincoat, a military army suit, and I had on a cowboy hat and cowboy boots. The police called me over and stopped me and told me I jaywalked. I said, "I'm not jaywalking, sir." He said, "You did jaywalk." He told me to come here and took my tickets. I kept walking, so he just grabbed me. Then all of a sudden, when he grabbed me, I said, "I haven't done anything." He told me to stay right here and then he called on his paddy wagon. They put me in the paddy wagon and told me I was soliciting or no, he just said I jaywalked. Jaywalked, that's what they put on there, jaywalked.

Jaywalking is not illegal in Chicago. After this, they wanted to arrest me, so I asked them, "What am I in here for?" He asked me my name, and I ask him again, "What am I in here for?" He said, "What's your damn name?" I said, "What am I in here for; I'm not telling you my name if I don't know what I'm in here for." He said, "I *ain't* got to tell you shit!" And I said, "well, I *ain't* got to tell you my name." Then the white man, he jumped up. It was two of them. He jumped up and he started hitting me, all I did is just throw my arm up. I had just got finished getting out of the military; I'm telling you, while in the military, they just showed you how to kill, seek and destroy, how to take care of yourself. Now why did that damn honkey put his damn hands on me, I don't know? At this time, I'm not having sex, so you know I'm cock strong, okay. All I did was pushed him over, he fell back and the other one jumped up. I pushed him over and that motherfucker fell back too.

They fell out of the wagon, the door opened up and all the rest of them motherfuckers out the back came and they got to blowing whistles, the horses came and everything; but I wasn't getting back in that damn wagon. They wasn't gone hurt me. Then they came and they kicked me on my legs, I act as if I was hurt and things, so they dragged me and put me in the police car. It was on record that I jaywalked.

I started thinking I'm gone be out in no time, you know, *blasé, blasé, blasé*. Now don't forget, I'm still in school and I'm staying at the YMCA, all my stuff is at the YMCA; my skates, every *thang*. They put me in jail took my picture and let me sit there for a while, and you know, I *ain't* call nobody and let them know I was in there cause, Uncle Luke was at home and Big Mama and them was up here.... So, I probably could've got out on a bond, but then I found out they had put me in there on murder. They told me my name was, Benny Clark, alias Ricky Davis.

Now have you, Benny Clark was my big sister's boyfriend. He was hard. He was a burglar. He was a murderer. He did his lil' thang. He had a rap sheet.

One time I was visiting, we had driver's license that didn't have pictures on them in Chicago. They just had these lil' flowers, pink and bluish lil' flowers on it, and it just had your name, so they had stolen my wallet, and this brother, he was running around with my I.D. because he was already wanted, I guess this is what happened. This is the only thing I can see why they would consider me as a murderer. I told the judge that my name is not Benny Clark, my name is Ricky Davis, and I told him, don't you all have a picture and fingerprints of this Benny Clark? They told me to shut up and threw my ass in jail.

They kept sending me back and forth to court and kept giving me this court appointed attorney, and they kept telling me to plead guilty and take an I-bond. I told them, plead guilty to what? I said I *ain't* murdered anybody and my name *ain't* Benny Clark; I didn't do *nothing*. They said I jaywalked and every time I come down there, I assaulted the police. Yes, I did this because I was only protecting myself. They say I'm a killer and that I should plead guilty and take the I-bond. They sent me back there, to the smaller jail over at 26th & California in Chicago. I knew everybody because they are from the block.

This is where they hide everybody at 26th & California. It is a vacation. Sometimes you would be there two and three years before you are seen waiting your turn. A lot of y'all don't understand when they put you in that County jail, this is to break you down. We can't just send you straight to Statesville or Pontiac. You know how much game you would have? Do you know that you would go down there and not give a fuck about *nothing*. You just start tearing motherfuckers off.

This is what they are saying, "See, I got to put you in these County jails to break you down so you'll learn how to follow directions. We beat you down slowly but surely; we'll put you in a little hole. We put you down there, we let the gangs beat you up because we gone take the TV from them and whoever started this, so now we gone have to just jump on you; we gone have to whip you, we told you to clean up and you didn't."

They started calling me a *Neutron*. A *Neutron* is somebody that's not in a gang. But everybody that was in there I knew them because I was able to go all over the city. They were the ones that danced with me, some of them been to school. I just had me a good life. You know what I'm saying.... I'm not mad at the world.

One day, I'm lying in there reading the Bible. This was the first time I got a chance to read my Bible. I had been in here for six months. I started reading from Genesis and went all the way to Revelations, and it was deep, it was so deep it let my time go past and when I finished it, this is when I got out of jail. As soon as I finished that last page was the day that I was released out of jail.

I'm not saying that because I read my Bible that I got out of jail. All I am trying to tell you is when I read that Bible, and the things they said that I had done, the fighting I had to do, and all the things of my past played over in my mind. I had to forgive so that I could move on.

Being in jail is a controlled environment. They tell you when to go to bed, when to go outside, when to work. All you do is lye around and go in circles. We also had to make commissary every now and then. There were times you were able to get visitors to come and see you. I didn't get any because I didn't call my family to let them know I was on lock down.

I probably could have gotten out, but I wanted to get everything straight especially that murder charge. If I would've taken this again, it would have followed me everywhere I went. I learned in the military that they could kill you with a pencil and a piece of paper. If I would've taken this I-bond, I would've messed around and would have been labeled as Benny Clark. Since my fingers prints were under Benny Clark and Ricky Davis, there was no way they would've kept that shit straight.

All I'm trying to say is try to take care of your business. If you don't take care of your business, you going to get whatever they want to give you. So, as we were going along, I stayed in there, here it is six months; the brothers up in the jailhouse started calling me I-bond, because I kept refusing.

This time it wasn't a white judge, it was a black judge up there. He allowed me to explain after he asked me, "What are you in here for young man?" I said, "They got me in here for jaywalking." I kept the papers up under my mattress and I showed the judge. He asked, "You been here this long?" "I keep trying to tell them my name was not Benny Clark, my name is Ricky Davis if you look in that paper and if that is Benny Clark's file, you'll find out that we don't look *nothing* alike.

He said, "Well, what is all these other charges?" I said, "I don't know what it is. If you notice, the charges were put on there after I had been in jail for a while now. So, if I would've got out, they could've said it was during that time because the paperwork would've got confused and lost and if I wouldn't have kept that piece of paper, it would've gotten lost. Because I was moved around so much since then, I can't even put my hand on a lot of these papers."

While I was in jail, they told me to clean up and because I was moving kind of slow, they sent some boys on me. I could've took that mop bucket and fucked their asses up, just busted their whole head wide open, but that would've put me down there a little longer. See that's what they do. They know you are going to protect yourself, so they will convince some boys to come and mess with you.

I put a lot of thought in to what happens. I would always go home and think about how my day went. So, I'm sitting there reading the Bible and they rolled on me, but I got close to the radiator. They hurt themselves more than they hurt me. They was kicking each other and hitting that pole. I didn't get swelled up or nothing.

Later on that night, they said, Disco. You know, I had my guns when I was in there, what they call guns when you are in jail. These are some gloves you can put on to box. Those were your guns. So, they said, "Disco, you want to body punch/body fight with these brothers? Don't hit in the face, you know, *blasé, blasé*." I said, "No problem, they *ain't* never seen me throw no hands, but you know I had my *guns* under the mattress." And I said, "Well, let me go get my guns and put them on."

Every last one of them, it was like about six of them that rolled on me. I got a chance to whip each one of them one at a time. And all of them had to go to the Medic. All of them had to go to the sick wall. I was breaking ribs on them mark ass motherfuckers. See, because that's what I like to do, I like to box. Then the head man that was sitting there, the Chief, who was in control of the pro boxers, and who kept everything in order in there, he said, "Disco, I didn't know you could throw your hands like that." I said, "Yeah, it's a lot of things you don't know about me."

I just don't be out here doing nothing, you know, like playing with them, because they didn't like for you just to be boxing around there and uh, uh, because that was another form of showing that you had control and power. If you were starting to whip everybody, it would seem as if you had some kind of control and power.

After I whipped them, I didn't have any more problems after that. And I would sing, the acoustics out in the hallway echoed the words with a nice melody.

In order to keep us in shape we had to lift up these buckets of water, do push-ups, sit-ups; and some type of exercise; that's why these brothers so big. What they do is break you down so bad that you'd be so glad to do something that you accept anything. I mean any kind of work; anything to get you to go somewhere or do something for somebody. You would do shit for cigarettes.

This is a form of breaking you down before you go to the big house before you go to the penitentiary; before you go to the pen. We got to break you down and make sure you're ready for us so you don't give us no problems when you get down there you be already conformed to what we need. So brothers, please check it out. It's more of us in the penal institution than in the higher learning institution.

Right now they're building more penal institutions than they are higher learning institutions. If you notice, they are going back to free labor. They're doing the chain gang. They're even trying to bring the chain gangs back here. They even put women on the chain gang because this is getting ready to go for free labor. This is the part of it where they're getting ready to cut off the ADC, and things of this nature.

The New World Order, the illuminati, all this is coming; all these are in books. I'm saying and it *ain't* just written by black people, so we don't want to hear about where you get all this. Is this all black stuff? No, no, no. White people are writing about this stuff too. All I'm asking you, who don't know the past, are bound to repeat it. All I'm asking you to do is start reading books. Start off slow. It might take you two to three months to read one book, but finish that book. And then you'll be surprised, you'll say to yourself: hey I completed that. Then you go and complete something else.

All this trying to live so fast and so hard, and don't know why you're living so fast and so hard for. Most of y'all carrying y'all parents because they're strung out but they don't know any better because they're in that madness. You don't have to do this.

I found out that when you are mad at everybody, you have this big rock on your chest, it feels like a big boulder, it hurts you so bad, that when you see these people, it hurt you and they're just smiling and they're just having fun. They don't give a fuck about you.

Take that burden off you and quit being so angry at the world and you just go on and function and watch how well you will feel. How well you will look. Anger is nothing but a slow death; it's like cancer; it eats you up. Then you know you run around with this madness on your face and somebody say, "Hi," to you and you don't even know how to respond. You know how we do this. I say something to you and you want to start fighting automatically. You're always on the defensive because this is how you've been trained. You're trained to just go off because you feel everybody just messing with you.

It's time for us to slow down, take a deep breath, and breathe and just look at it. I didn't say just look at part of the picture, look at the whole picture, step back. Look at it. You'll find out, this is nothing, this is small. This is very small. The stuff that you're getting upset about and the people that are making you upset is very small also. All I'm trying to tell you, you don't have time for this. You got to keep going forward. All I'm asking you is to quit carrying our parents, quit worrying about what your parents did to you. Is there any way you can correct it? No. Learn from it even if it is evil and bad.

I didn't say put yourself in immediate danger, I did not say that. I did not say if you see yourself about to be killed, or you going to be hurt, that you suppose to sit there and continue to take this. All I'm asking is that we teach our kids to recognize dangers and the danger signs when they see it. Recognize your enemy. Your enemy is anyone who's trying to do you physically and mentally harm. They can come in any shape and size.

We don't want this to be like, this is anti-white, this is anti-this, no, no. I am not going there. It's time to get passed that. Know your enemies and if you can hear what I'm telling you, when I tell you to know your enemies, that's all I'm going say. Now watch they pick out something and say that I have done something else wrong. But I'm not worried about that; I'm dead already.

What do you do with a dead man? I leave him alone. What I got to worry about? They've done everything to me imaginable that could be done to a human. I'm still going, I'm still going. Things would even get better for me.

Alright, after I get out of the jail thing, I come back to school and finish at Malcolm X college, and it took me a while. It was off and on; I was staying with friends and things, until I finished and I finally graduated.

CHAPTER TEN

During this time, I met my wife, we were doing parties at Bailey's and we were doing house parties. Now have you, I don't drink or get high or none of that, this is an all-natural party, like it is now; like it is till this day - I got a natural high.

I graduated from Malcolm X, and I got recruited to go to Stillman, in Tuscaloosa, Alabama; which I accepted, and I went down there for only one semester, because my wife, she's a vet, as I call her got pregnant, although I didn't want her to get pregnant. She said she couldn't get pregnant, and I don't have any kids out there, except this one that I know of.

I graduated, kicked it with her for a while, and right before it was time for me to go on down there to Stillman, she told me she was pregnant, but I already had agreed that I would go down there, so I go down there, and Stillman was a different place.

Stillman in Tuscaloosa, Alabama, is a Lutheran college; it was different. So, I go and pass. Then they sent me over to Alabama State. And over here at Stillman, King came down through there. He attended.

This is the same place where they allow the Tuskegee Institute to study Syphilis. It is a book out that is called "The Bad Blood--Nurse Rivers study." You know the government gave it to them and let them study Syphilis. They act like they were curing them and all along they misled them; like they do everything.

Like I always say, just know your enemy, I *ain't* saying nothing wrong with nothing or this, when I say enemy, anything that is going to hurt you, so we don't put names on it or whatever. Anything that's hurting you, it can be considered as an enemy. Not just because you think it's hurting you; it's actually hurting you. You know it's causing confusion and havoc, because that's the job, to keep up confusion and madness; ever since it's been here; confusion and madness. Anytime we all get together, ain't no confusion and madness; it's harmony. But soon as you throw that monkey in there, its divide and conquer, the infamous Willie Lynch Letter, we fall apart.

Jessie Jackson came through there and did his little speech; and one of the Kennedy boys came through and did his speech, when we were down there. It was another way of me seeing the United States. I have seen a lot of the United States. When I was in the service, they sent me under guard to Graphenvere in Germany U.S. base. They wouldn't let me walk around over there. It wasn't nothing but a big ghetto. It was just white people-Europeans living like in the ghetto because that was the *thang*. They loved some black man; they loved them some black women too. But everybody seemed to dislike us everywhere when they get here to the United States. Oh, when you go to their country, they look out for you. Soon as they get here, they know how to say the "N" word. They see us as bad! They know this is all they see us. Now when we go over to their country, they want to touch you, they want to get close to you because they haven't been taught this yet.

When I get down there to Stillman, they were still flying the Confederate flag. It was okay, they could still call you the "N" word, it was certain places you could go-I went to some club, and I was dancing, you know, we thought we were having a good time, and they came up to me and told me just like this, *(in his old southern accent)* "You know boy, you new around here *ain't* you?" Yeah, they say. "You don't know what you doing here, do you? We don't allow you to be dancing with our girls, but we gone let you dance this time, but we won't have this anymore and you shouldn't really come down this way again. I understand you don't know. Do you understand what I'm saying to you?" I mean he was a real hillbilly. He was a real hillbilly; him and his boys.

All I did was stopped dancing right then and I got the hell up out of there; I didn't have to be there. You don't have to explain to me what. Down there, at least they will tell you they don't like you. Up here, they smile at you and cross you out. Like I say, just know, and be aware and go with your instincts; go with your gut feelings and don't be scared to deal with it.

Now, after we get finished with that and I come back up here and my wife is pregnant, I had to get here, I had to work like three and four jobs just to make it so we can get finished because we couldn't take care of the baby, you know like, when she was getting ready to have the baby, she had to get on ADC and everything. They were treating her, you know, all bad, asking where I was at. You know I was right here, I was back at school, here I am. You can see me. You know, but they make you feel bad, you got to go in there and tell them about where your man is at, how he is doing. Again, we going back to that divide and conquer. They give her the money, but they won't give it to you. If she is staying with you, then she can't have it.

Again, late 50's, early 60's ADC, welfare, Aide For Women with Dependent Children, it's doing the same *thang*, again—Same game, different name. Game recognizes game. They haven't changed that much from what it has been. Again, a people who do not know his past, is bound to repeat it. You will repeat it.

She got pregnant again the next year and a half later, got pregnant again. You know, I'm still not making it, I'm living with them. I didn't have *nothing* when I asked her father if I could marry her. I married her before we had the baby. I asked him could I stay there because I didn't have *nothing*. I explained to him my situation. I was working around, doing anything, janitor work, cutting grass, anything just to make it. I did want to have kids. I grew up like this though-but since I got them, I'm glad I had them. Since they are here, I have to deal with them.

I tried to go back to school, and then I finally got a job in transportation, and I've been there now for 12 years, so I quit going to school. It wasn't until 12 years later that I went back to school. It's a whole different set. A lot of the brothers and sisters that I have encountered are living so large and so slick. They have everything so they are not even taking it seriously.

What I'm finding out, there are still forces among our own who would try to hurt you. I had to explain to a few of them, I'm going to school now because I want to; not because I have to, so you can't be threatening me about what you gone do or how you gone fail me and how you gone do this and how you gone do that.

See when they came up, they still using that big power stick *thang*. And you know, this is a higher learning institution, we should know better. And then it's, some of that stuff that they're teaching us, they do what they tell us we're not supposed to do. It's certain classes, they teach you one way that come straight out the book, what they supposed to do, and they don't even know how to adapt themselves to what they're teaching you. This would make you think that this will really work great in this society.

A lot of stuff we learn in school, we will not use in the real world. All of these are controlled environments. In the real world, it's all the way different, it's a whole different way of doing things; it's a whole different party. We have to be ready at all times. You have to learn all that you can. You should never stop learning. No matter what anybody tells you, you can't do. If you feel like you can, try it.

You have these notions of the American dream, and a husband and your house, the car, the two kids, the dog, the fish and all the furniture that you may want to have. Well during this particular time, that's what I was telling you about when I was telling you earlier about being a vet and receiving these benefits. I had already had it in my mind because I had watched them all through the time how hard it was just for them to get a house; or to get a down payment for a house. Now, the American dream, that's exactly what it is, you *gonna* have to be sleep in order to deal with it, because if you're wide awake, you would not be able to deal with this American dream.

The American dream is not what you think it is. The American dream is dealing with bills, finance, economic, things of this nature. They tell you the American dream is the American dream, but it's not. And the American dream is not what they say it is. It is hard work. You have to constantly do what you have to do. Like over these 12 years that I was out of school, I was able to work and I purchased the house, in the suburbs, coming from the ghetto, I was not supposed to come this far, I should have been dead by now, or either in jail, or not even thinking about these things.

My life was supposed to have been so consumed with just trying to survive and just trying to make it, that we need to do more to try to make it where it could fit our needs, instead of just trying to survive. Instead of trying to survive should be over with by now. If I had never been a veteran, I would not be allotted the opportunity I have today. Even with my kids going to school today and my first wife, they still have a hard time as far as trying to make ends meet.

They would tell my children you attend a Lutheran school now. The color of the cross is brown which is considered bad because that is what they hung Jesus on. Black is considered as bad, darkness. Even the way they set up colors, your subconscious teach you that the darker the color, the worst the situation you're in. So, this whole format has been done for years and years and years and it have been integrated into our system. Even till this day, we have more or less a system that will hinder you and will train you how to act and how to think.

The way they have our rappers fighting each other, and all of them are living the same type of life, they're living the life that I just told you about. But what they're doing, they're putting it on wax. As I had told you earlier about how they were gang banging. They're gangbanging on wax. It's time to stop, bring your finances all together.... I found out that every nationality can teach our own people, but every time we get together and get ready to teach our own, it's madness.

Every culture has its own higher learning institution; each culture has its own banking system. A lot of these cultures are able to become global, international. But we as black Americans, here in the United States, we can't even open up our own schools, our own hospitals, teach our own kids. Soon as we do, there's some kind of resistance. When they see that you're doing what you supposed to do, even your own, especially your own female tends to have an attitude. This is something. We have work to do.

Once the sister finds out she's the mother of the world, she will quickly change her attitudes, because they're constantly using her till this day. Most Europeans use the sisters to keep his books in order. We on the other hand do not always have the necessary tools in place to do what is needed.

Our sisters don't even recognize us because we cannot take them out to a fine restaurant for dinner, but that's something we have to deal with. I hope that the sisters will soon recognize that the black male is very tired. He's very tired of carrying her. She thinks she is carrying us, we are carrying her. This is the only reason she's in the position she's in till this day. Also, what I would like to say is that, I've been out here for a while now, and a lot of us still don't realize that we are still being somewhat discriminated against. I'm not saying by everybody, or all, whatever.... But all I ask for you to do is quit talking about we're trying to make an excuse.

Step back! Step back and see how hard it was for you to do whatever it is you're trying to do and how many times you've been hindered and stopped. Life is like that. Ever since we have been little, it's been like that. As you get older and you put in the work and you do everything else, you are still hindered and stopped to a certain extent.

You can take it in any fashion or any way you will like to take this, but just stop, step back and see how many times you've been somewhere and been stopped because you've progressed, or you were progressing. Then you will tell me that, no, this *ain't* happened. I put on the blinders a lot of times too, but this is a natural fact and we must recognize this. Everybody else can teach their own and have their own institutions, schools, hospitals, and everything else, but we do not have this.

If you think there is something wrong with what I said in the previous paragraph, stop, step back and ask the; question why? When you come up with the answer to why, you will find out it's nothing that you did, it's just an *all-out* war against you. Do not use this as a handicap; use it as a tool to continue striving for the best. Know that it's there so when you get there you won't be totally disappointed, because I see a lot of people that breaks out of these higher learning institutions, especially of my race; that really struggled, and once they get there, they find out it is not nice at all. It's nothing near what they were taught and when they get out in the real world, the real world usually tear them off.

A lot of them are career soldiers, career this and career that, because they could not make it out in the real world. When you get into that prison system, it's real hard for you to come out into the real world and function; you can't function once you've been in there. I'm not going to say all but some can't function once they've been institutionalized. They have to keep going back. I have relatives and kin folks that go back regularly then when they get out here, the world is just too hard for them as far as trying to pay their bills, and taking care of the family, it's just too hard; they're bound to destroy something. Most of them are out here trying to be slick, but they end up getting tricked. They try to be so slick; how are they goin' to beat the system.

Our babies are on this medicine now, just to receive ADC. It's the same flavor; you doing anything you can just to take care of your habit, so that means you're not really thinking about the kids. Your kids will grow up and be labeled as educationally handicapped and then you wonder why he can't pass his grades; why Johnny can't read? He's already not being taught how to read in the neighborhood. Also what used to trip me out, I had some classmates that went to school with me, and they would come to my house in the morning before they went to school to shoot some dope; I used to watch them, and they used to wonder why I wasn't doing it. I grew up with it, why should I have to do it?

On my Mother's side of the family, some of them thought they were better than us; they didn't even associate themselves with us. That's alright though.... My Grandmother on my Mother's side didn't care for my Father at all. Like I had mentioned earlier, a lot of these entertainers, like the rappers had no economic background either. They did not know. They do not know what to do with the money, how to use money.

We would go out and buy a car, material things, before we even buy a house. The system has it so, where it's so much red tape for you to even invest your money back into the community where you can make a profit. Everyone else can come and make a profit, but you can't make a profit.

If you try to get through our environment, the roughness and the hardness that we get, it's the same way, you reach this wall or you have to stop. And, the same way when they get into this big entertainment field. I'm not just calling any names, but a lot of them, they can open up a bank but you know how much red tape that would be to open a bank; to open a grocery store—chain of food; to open a hospital; and to open anything that's dealing with having a healthy mind and body where we can provide for ourselves. It's literally impossible for most.

I can count on one of my hands the number of us who owns a professional sports team. If those guys that are making the millions and millions and millions of dollars try to bring our money together, we will see how fast they'll stop it. At that point, we can take this money and lend it out to us at a lower rate than what the bank would charge us, which will bring the community money back since we supposed to have the largest bunch of money. Again, we're not taught this, we are not supposed to see this.

Even when we were little, they would let their kids play with us while they're little, like even now today. It's a few Caucasian people in the neighborhood that would let their kids play with us, but when they get bigger they find other things for them to do. For instance, swimming, outdoor activities, camp, connect them with certain groups like Cub Scouts.

When they notice we start participating, they would take their kids out the group and put them somewhere else. This is teaching the kids prejudice, unconsciously. Then they would go home and teach them and tell them something because the kid would say something that will come out of his mouth that you know it only had to come from a parent. This is the problem we have been dealing with all of our lives.

Then we have certain teachers that they would send down to our community that would not be concern about us learning. They were scarred of us from *jump street*. It would be some little young new white girl just coming out of college and they would put her down there; and then she feels some kind of sympathy for us as if she has to do this. Then when she teaches us and the system finds out, they remove her.

They just wear us down.... Slowly but surely.... And we keep going for it. Just like these big corporations and banks who have invested in these prisons and jails just like they did shopping malls. We're getting ready to get free labor and then it's a lot more black females going to jail now also. The women are doing things that they would never do. You see a lot of black females leaving their babies now; killing their babies; just doing a whole bunch of madness; because they're trying to mimic them. Again, this whole setup is on material things.

When you find out you're looking for the American dream, a lot of times it turns out to be an American nightmare. Now, I'm not putting it down ... I've done a lot of travelling so far, and I'm still travelling. Every country I've been to, they're poorer than us. I would be happy when I get back here, but this is the way the system has it, this is what our United Nations is all about. They control, they can destroy or build or whatever they want to, whatever is in their interest, that's what they would do just like with the CIA and everybody else that we can't trust.

I'm not just calling out just to be calling out. All I'm asking is, or saying nothing bad about them, so we won't have any problems with this. All I'm asking you to do is do a little bit of reading and some investigation on your own and then use your common sense, ask for wisdom, knowledge and understanding. Just like I've read the Jewish Torah, the Holy Koran, and the Holy Bible, I've read these things numerous times, and all of them are saying the same thing, so why are we fighting?

Just like I've been back and forth to a lot of different churches, and a lot of people that were in church, were worse than the people that they degrade who supposed to be out there on the streets. We find more bad people in the church than we do outside the church. I'm not saying all of them but some of them. Church is a business. All of us fall under the same realm, or they would destroy it. I've said all of this just to say, let's do better than what we have been doing. I'm not a genius but I can talk to the poorest of the poorest or the richest of the richest; the elite of the elite, the highest of the highest. I feel like there shouldn't be too much of a struggle, but it has to be there in order to keep us divided and conquered and keep our mind off the big picture.

They give us little problems, take away our little ADC, take away our little SSI, give a little here, take a little there, give you this, say you *gotta* have this in order to be considered as normal or that you have reached the route of passage. Are you able to move up in the world? You have to do a number of things in order to bring this combination together to make yourself feel like a success and if you miss any of these steps, you'll feel like a looser to a certain extent. If you don't know how to deal with it instead of continuing on because you're *gonna* make mistakes because you're only human, they will shut you down. You can't be perfect, because if you were, hey, that's a whole *nother* level. Just be human and know that you're going to make failures but there are forces that are set out there to hinder you and stop you; but once you fall, you'll get back up.

I tell my son all the time, if he falls and hurt himself, he can cry. All that macho-man stuff about this-'n'-that; you can't cry and you got to be the man; you got to be the dominant species is not good to teach our sons. If you notice, this is almost turning out to be a woman's world. This is what they're fighting, just like they're fighting against us, they fighting against women, because if you all step up to your place, I still haven't seen a man have a baby yet. I have seen women have babies, so a lot of this evolution thing about man came first; not just evolution but, a lot of stuff that's been written about man came first and then woman, and not the other way around; a lot of times we have to stop and think, so, let's just try to see if we can bring these forces together.

I have a lot of problems with a lot of us; especially our sisters. I'm not saying all of them. A lot of us brothers tend to have blinders on that we don't even want to see the real world; we don't even want to recognize it. Then when we do, you get upset because you had got so comfortable with it and you're doing so well, that you scarred of being poor again.

This is what they do with a lot of these entertainers that are well-to-do brothers and sisters, they can threaten them by saying you didn't pay your taxes, or you didn't do something. They would pit us against each other, first you say you love me so much you do anything I say, and then when they bust me and they come at you, you just turn the whole script around. Because they threaten to take your family, they threatened to put you in jail and you never been there before.

It's really hard to be poor. Then do well, then do very well and above very well and then to be told that they can reduce you back down to nothing. Well, this is part of the conscious, self-conscious, scariness that we don't want to do. Then when certain conversations come up, we run from them. We won't even confront them; we won't even want to hear them.

He is just messed up in the head, something wrong with him. First he says, you just looking for an excuse; you just doing this. But if you're in the real world, you're not looking for any excuses; the excuse is right here on you. You are supposed to step to the left and try to deal with it but recognize it, teach your kids, teach yourselves don't ever stop learning. I'm just here and I hope that I will be able to come back again and give you some more information, but I feel like everybody has something to say, and we have to be careful what we hear or what we accept. All I ask you to do is, take out the parts that you need inside the pages of this book, and adjust it to the way your life is. See what you can implement in your life a lot better than what you have. Set it up so you can deal with it a little bit better; in some kind of sane order.

Let me ask you this, did you fall apart because you weren't prepared? Or, is it because, once you did become prepared, it shocked you? When I started doing a lot of reading of different kinds of information that I came across, it could drive you insane. It can put you in the hospital. It could make you lose your mind, just like a lot of entertainers, they get out in the field and then they change and want to turn religious getting involved with some different kind of religion that they don't know anything about because they were scarred. A lot of times if you're an entertainer, male or female, you think you got to turn gay or lesbian because you're not in....

Another thing, I found out that it's so difficult for a man with children to receive public assistance, even if the mother abandoned the kids and left them with the father. They make it very difficult for a man, especially a black man to receive any assistance if he really came to apply for his kids and try to get assistance, the system is set up so good where it's for women with dependent children, not men with dependent children, so I guess we really don't exist out here in this world.

I've been noticing that even when my Father used to have us on public assistance, they would send him through so many changes. Nowadays, they would send the sister to school making sure she gets some form of education. These sisters have been in the system for generations and generations. I'm talking about, let's say about, three generations that I know that have received public aid, but are now working their way out of the system. The system is in place to make them go to school or work for their check.

A male cannot go through all these channels because they send them through so many changes as if they abandon their children. This is double standards between men vs. women. Now the women are getting the jobs, the marketplace is opening up for more women to enter into the workforce because a lot of the white males are leaving the workforce, they're getting older. They're going to have to use women and minorities, and immigrants to fill these jobs, because we're going into a service oriented country. Women are getting the jobs.

I'm not saying anything bad about them, but they're getting the jobs and then they don't want to perform and then they will put you in jail. This is free labor; it is going to be free labor. Pretty soon, the streets should be clean because they're going to take the ones out of prison they're going to clean these streets. The city streets are going to be clean, and be well protected. You are just going to jail, lye there, and get three meals, and then put you in a hole when you act bad.

If you separate a man from himself for a while, he tends to adjust; you can go stir crazy. It's very difficult for you to come out in the real world after you've been penalized all your life you know nothing but the prison system. You have to go back. You cannot function out here in this world. Again, I'm not mad at the female, I'm glad they're moving up, but it's just a double standard.

There are not too many of us black men out here on the streets. Then most of the time if you notice, even the ones in the projects, when they live in the projects, they can't run over nothing but their shoes. They can't run their house, they can't run nothing because when her check comes, she gets this big high head about herself and then she would go and buy these fingernails, the hair, the eyes lashes, and everything, and put the man out during the time when she has the money. Then when the money is gone, he can come back in and service her let's just say, service her. Then once he gets finished servicing her, she'll put him out and then somebody else will pick him up and he'll service her girlfriend, or her friend or sister or whoever. Then they'll get pregnant and this is how that madness continues on where we're still in the studding stage like we were when we were slaves.

The system used to be against gay men. It was against the law to state that you were gay although they didn't really talk against being lesbians, because you know ... they even show you today that it's okay for two women to be together more than it is for two men to be together. They frown on two men, but mostly feel two women together is the norm. It's like cool. It's a big double standard.

Women are still running stuff now, we can say what we want to say about they're being underpaid. If they had the same job a man has, especially if it's a blue collar job like the police, the fire department, the mailman, bus driver, anything of that type, they're making just as much money as we're making. All that about they're not making it and they can't do this is not true.

Some are coming out of the houses now because it takes two incomes to raise a family. We fight with who's the boss of the house. We really do not have to go through who's the boss, that's what I have to say about the subject. I try not to struggle on who is the boss, because I see you as an equal. I'm not your father, I'm not your mother and I'm not trying to be none of this because we are here as a team. The family system has been destroyed.

You can't even punish your kids for ditching school. You can't punish your kids for stealing, you can't punish your kids for hurting somebody, and you can't punish your kids for anything. So, they end up on the street slinging drugs buying their parents Mercedes, microwaves, furniture, clothes, and buying food. What they are actually doing are buying their parents. The parents become so weak that they go ahead and accept this kind of behavior. Now the kids run the house. The parents just have to sit there and take a lot of this abuse, and this hardship, while the kids do what they have to do to survive the street life.

When I say beat the kids, I'm talking about, whipping them. I am not talking about beating them to death or killing them or nothing like that. If you beat your kids, they'll take them and put them in foster homes. People who whip their kids, they beat them, and then if they get locked in the penal institution, he's going to beat them to death. He's going to beat him down until he submits to the rules and regulations. You can't do this, so you better tell your kid, I can't beat you, but they're going to beat you. They *gonna* beat you down! It's set up like this, they tell you one thing, they do another thing. It's just like that, and that's the way we grew up, and I watched that.

They give the kids a child abuse hotline, the kids telling you what you can't do, kids all up in your face calling their parents bitches, whores, motherfuckers. Telling them I'll kick your ass! Some of these kids are kicking their parents' asses. They're whipping their parents. The parents have no parent abuse center. They probably got them, but like I say, they're far and few.

Then when you call the police on the kids, it means you're part of the system. You showed them that, I can't do anything with my children. You ask the police to take them. They'll take them from you alright.... Once they get finished with them, they'll never be any good any more. Once they get into the system, it's hard to get out. Once you get caught in the systems.... Like we've been a part of the system for so long, it's hard to get out. We think it's a norm. We think that we supposed to get ADC; we suppose to get SSI; we suppose to get some kind of assistance.

Now what they're doing is put you on SSI, and you have to say in order for you to get it that they sent you through this channel. You had to say you were on drugs or an alcoholic, you were this or you were that, you couldn't read, you couldn't function in society, then they will give you SSI. Now they're getting ready to take it back. As I mentioned earlier, it is more white people and foreigners on ADC and SSI than it is of us. What we need to do is, calm down, step back and get ready to adjust ourselves to this situation.

Also I noticed that when our sisters get mad at us, they can call the police and say that we hit them even if we didn't. The police put you out your own house to tell you to go for a walk and she might've been wrong, she might've been there doing whatever she wanted to do. She was wrong as two left feet and she hit you and now you're standing there afraid to tell someone. If my wife ever hit me, we really need to be separated. But if your woman hit you, call the police on her. You have just as many rights as she does. It's time to turn the script around. It's time for you to cry. She wants the kids, you want the kids. What makes her so different from you if you're doing the same thing she's doing, we should be placed on the same level.

Nowadays, most women aren't taking care of the kids, it's the men taking care of the kids, look at it, especially in our community. We're Mister Moms. Our women are gone or they're so busy trying to reach their careers and their goal, that they don't cook no more, they don't clean no more, you find yourself doing these things -- you find yourself picking the kids up from school, taking them to school, bringing them back, and all she is really doing is giving you some sex.

Look at it now, she's not giving you money, some of you guys getting money, but you know, you're considered as a stud. The majority of us are just getting some sex. We're sitting there and we are supposed to be happy with this. If you look at it, it's more females out here than it is males. If we do what we are supposed to do, it will turn back around.

I'm not saying all of them, a lot of them go with their girlfriends because they don't want to be with us. She can't run *nothin'* here. We can't do nothing but run over our own shoes in our house. Our kids tell us what to do, because they gave her the SSI, ADC, and you're not bringing in anything, even if you worked at McDavids, she still wouldn't have been satisfied.

Before he is able to give her a lot of different things, material things, she doesn't want you. It's bad when a large percentage of our women will go to another race instead of being with us because they will provide for them. The other race will take them out to dinner, dress them, then when they find themselves not happy and satisfied, they want you to creep with them; they want you to be their boyfriend again. All this stuff because they went out of the race.

Another point I would like to make is some of the sisters look like Queen Latifah, queen everything, queen this. She really is but she is not black. I call her sister Crossover and brother Oreo. That's the way it goes, you know, instead of calling them Uncle Toms, I call them crossovers. I'm not mad at them and we are not going to be fighting against them because we need everything we got.

You might say that I'm talking negative about gays, lesbians and stuff like that, but when we get further along, we are going to need everything we got. It might be a gay person that knows accounting, he might be a good lawyer, a lesbian person that might be a great attorney, she can do all kinds of things, so we don't need to be fighting against them. We will have to come together and be as one.

What we would do is ask them to let the buck stop where they're at. It's somebody out there that like doing what they're doing, but don't introduce it to one of our kids or take them back into that madness; stay with your bunch;

stay with those who think that is normal. But don't go out here recruiting our kids and turning them out. Parents again, you should let your kids see the real world, because if you're living a great life and you're living in the suburbs and you're black or whatever you are. I don't care. I would even say whatever color you are, take them out and let them see the real world. Let them see the prostitutes out there selling themselves at night; the dope fiends, the alcoholics, the bums. Let them see this; let them see the raggedy parts of the city. Don't always take them down to the museum or something; the Science of Industry, because when they get out here and their friends introduce it to them, they are going to think it's cool. They're going to think that because it's different, it's okay. They never seen this, they never heard this language; when they start treating them real bad. They've been used to having everything given to them on a silver platter, then when they get out here, this un-never seen or never felt feeling will come on them and they will think it's something new and this is how our kids get strung out on dope and want to hang out with the rough ones and you'll be like; well she came from a good neighborhood; he came from a good neighborhood. What it is, you trying to hide them from the real world. The real world is waiting out there for them.

You give them a false sense of what life is, and it's not like that. When they get out here it's a whole different ballgame. So please, do not keep them sheltered do not cheat your kids. If you're black, teach your kids about their history. It's books out there all day long. I *ain't* saying to teach them how to be prejudice or anything; I am saying try to give them a well-balanced sense of study, especially about their history.

We just got back from Africa, not too long ago; we went to Egypt. Everything that's written on those pyramid walls are written in the Jewish Torah, the Holy Qur'an, the

Holy Bible and so on and so forth. They use it for their own purpose. They took out only what they wanted and used it. So it's not nothing new; it's not nothing new. Just like what I'm saying now, it's been written and said somewhere before, by someone else. My words are being regurgitated, being reused and re-done again. When you take this book, I hope that you will be able to get something out of here that adapts to your life, because I found out that misery likes company.

Sometimes you deal with a female that's nowhere near your level or your league. Same way with women, she deals with a man, who's nowhere near her level or league as far as education, lifestyles and all this, and they might have some good sex-yeah, y'all might be having good sex, but you have nothing else in common. Your goals are different, her attitude is different, his attitude is different; the way you dress, the way you do things find something that you have in common, or see that you all will be able to have an open line of communication where you won't be fighting all the time, especially about money.

It gets so bad that this is what really destroys us, we are so worried about the material things that we don't even recognize love anymore; love is just a word now. We don't even know what it is. It's just a plain, everyday word. I-Love-You; I-Love-You-Too. But what I'm trying to tell you is that all through my life it's been ups and downs, even till this day, I'm still scared to give my all-n-all; because you end up so disappointed. People will disappoint you. So if you learn how to conquer yourself and love yourself when these tragedies come, you'll be able to deal with it.

You will ask yourself questions as: what if this would happen? How will I handle this? What if this will happen? How will I handle that? What if that will happen? How will I handle this? Look at the good and the bad, look at the pros and the cons of everything, even your relationship, so when it happens you won't snap; you will not hurt somebody; you will just be able to walk away. It's going to hit you. But you'll be able to step on and continue on with your life.

You don't have to be stalking people and people stalking you and so and so forth.... You learned this off of TV. You know, I understand you care about a person so much, but let them go if they want to be, let them go; it's someone else out there for you.

In a relationship, both parties know when they are wrong. You are aware of everything you say, everything you did, everything you stole, everybody you've been with. You cannot lie to yourself. Every time you look in the mirror, you'll see you. There is nobody else there with you. A lot of times you just sit down and when everybody is gone and nobody is there but you, you think about what you did; I bet you can remember everything you did, everything.

I'm not a saint and I'm not going to try to be one, because once I go there, they are going to find something wrong with me. If this book does what it supposed to do, watch how my words will be turned around, or how they'll analyze everything. They've already done that to me. I go left; they tell me I was supposed to go right. I go up; they tell me I was supposed to go down. I try to better myself then they tell me I am not good enough.

For this reason, you have to deal with who you are. They even said to me that I don't like people. They will have a mental physician do an analyses on me who do not have children and who do not know me from Adam or a housecat that will conclude that I am somewhat twisted in my thinking.

We even let the media and everybody tell us who we are instead of us using our own minds. This is a form of control, and this is intended to keep us in a mode of dependency. It is similar to the Infamous Willie Lynch Letter. Trust nobody but me; you believe what I tell you; don't believe what someone else tells you. If we keep going with this program, we'll never be able to see people for who they are or what's real and what's counterfeit, and what is artificial.

Again, if you notice, most of our athletes and entertainers are taken straight out of our neighborhood and they are placed in a zone where they don't even see their own kind. It's hard for them to come back, they feel they do not belong or fit in. I want to tell them, you will fit in because this is where you came from. You probably feel that you are doing so well that you can't even go back to your old neighborhood.

A lot of people will see this book and probably figure out who I'm talking about and who's this and who's that... But I'm leaving their names out and the only reason I will leave their names out is because if you come to me with a whole bunch of nonsense you will see I'm from the streets, you know me; you know where I'm at. If you come to me with this nonsense, all you are going to do is expose yourself, when you start telling me that this is that and while you do this, I'm not giving your name.

All I'm asking you is, take this book and look at it, read it and hopefully you can even smile at some of the places and things I'm saying in this book. If you can smile at it that means you're learning from it. If not, you disagree with it wholeheartedly.

I used to do that all the time. I even make a joke out of certain things that were hard in our lives. We just laughed although we knew what was serious. It's a whole different world. It's the same world, but the times changed what we are going to accept and what we're not going to accept.

There is a system in place of who's going to do this and who's going to do that? They even pick this person against that person. Another game that is played, if I keep up a lot of confusion, you really have no time to figure out exactly what I'm doing. I was telling somebody the other day that they have *think tanks*, people who think 200 years into the future. We don't have it like that, we are not thinking on that level; we just think about the general area here 10/20 years into the future, if that.

They already went where we want to go. They've already put it on the computer and have done the math. If we have this many people in the world then this is the amount of land that the people cover. Counting the amount of people a question arose, how can we feed all these people? Then the Pope tells us to keep having babies. Then a statement is made, we are not going to have enough money to be able to feed these people. We are going to become extinct like dinosaurs. All we are trying to do is function from day-to-day. We do not have a *think tank*.

We as an African American race don't have any higher learning institutions that we can call our own; institutions where we can teach our own and taught by our own where all you see is African American people.

When you attend the public school system, you see more females than males. You will also see more female teachers verses male teachers, especially a black male teacher that's not gay. Some are not gay, but the majority of them that are gay were placed in front of me when I was coming up. They were not teaching us, they actually liked the little boys if you know what I mean. They all were not like that but the majority of them were. If little black boys saw that only gay people are smart then he's going to want to be gay. This was the image that was displayed in front of us. He is not going to want to be like me believing that being straight is unintelligent.

If they're being hard and getting beat down—because I watched a lot of older guys that had a lot of kids, they broke them down; they broke them down. And then a lot of kids grew up to be shitheads, because their father's was so busy working that he didn't have time to really be with the kids.

What I did since I had kids, I just slowed down. For these last 12 years, I've been Mr. Mom like a big dog. You know you might catch me cleaning up the house, taking the kids to the Cub Scouts/Girl Scouts; I'm doing this and doing that with the other kids, or doing community service and things of this nature.... You would be surprised how some kids see you and then again they don't. But I'm gone tell you something, somebody always see you doing something. If they don't see you doing anything, they will invent something that you did. They will say, "I saw him, I saw him do that too, yeah I saw him." But like I say, don't worry too much about that.

All I'm asking everybody to do, whoever reads this book, is to sit back, think about your life and try to better yourself for yourself. Not for anybody else, not for your kids, not for your wife, not for your preacher, not for this or that. Because a lot of us, when we go to these churches expecting to receive sympathy, we get the opposite. Like when they catch you in a depressed mood, catch you when you're down, there's nothing going good for you, your luck is the pits, you haven't slept in days, you don't know where your next meal is *gonna* come from, and you don't know this or that, this is when the church starts using things against you.

If you notice, mostly all the women are in church. You don't find too many brothers in church; you find a lot of *gumps* in church; you find a lot of gay people in church; a lot of everything in church--all those Miss Nosey-bodies, the big hat wearing women, sitting up in the front, trying to trick somebody.

They get up in there, and some of the brothers that are going to these churches are going for business. They are already dope fiends or strung out or something and they catch these sisters up in there that's sitting there trying to look cute spending all their money and what they got is on their back, just like the brothers do out here in these streets, but they doing it in church.

They're sitting there with all these big hat business, and then they hook up with this man that looks like he's the best thing in the world, they really don't know him. He has been a criminal all his life. He's a dope dealer, a slick boy, a hustler. Then when she gets him, they get married and *thangs*. Then all this ugliness comes out; she finds out he is a dope fiend. She finds out he's never worked, he has just been going around and around and around. She is so happy not focusing on what he is really doing.

Once she finds out, she starts bringing herself up by getting an education at the same time sinking into a state of depression because of what she has gotten herself in to. She starts believing that it was the institution that helped her get to where she is. It really wasn't the institution. It was God. There is no way to make it without God.

She knows when she was going through that depressed mode, or when she was in that depressed feeling, she couldn't do anything, she felt helpless. She didn't want to eat, didn't want to comb her hair, and didn't want to do anything. She knows because it was a shock, it was devastating.

I don't know, whatever the shock might be that put you in that position, I don't know what it is, you can take your choice of the litter, because if I pinpoint it down to one thing—well, that ain't me. I'm gone tell you just like this, take your choice of the litter, whatever the situation is that got you depressed to bring you down like that, once you go to church and you straighten yourself up, because you have some kind of goal, some kind of focus, some kind of direction to go in, you'll think that institution did it and it wasn't, it was yourself.

CHAPTER ELEVEN

In dealing with the public, I see a lot. For instance, black males and females outside on the street waiting around in the cold respecting and a fat, *stankin'* white person while disrespecting one another. A black male will disrespect a sister and respect a white woman; then a black female will give a white man more respect than she does a brother.

Blacks will step back and let this Caucasian person step to the front, while they stand out there being cold and being polite to him, but are not polite to each other. I still haven't figured that out yet till this day. I have seen a white man who didn't look like anything and the sister was just smiling at him, had her teeth all hanging out and *thangs*.... I've seen a brother do the same *thang*, the white girl didn't look like anything, he was just smiling and falling all down for her, and then when a sister came that was gorgeous and a brother came and was handsome, had something on the ball, she rolled her eyes at him--he turned his nose up at her, like she did something to him-or she's done something to him or he's done something to her. We treat everybody else like gold.

All these foreigners coming to America opening businesses in our neighborhoods got our daughters pregnant. We got lil' Arab babies running around in the neighborhood now, they look mostly black, but the sister gave away some sex for some cigarettes or some pampers or whatever. Here it is a brother that has a job that might be able to do something for her, she wouldn't even recognize him, she's tired of our race telling brothers, you can't do *nothing* for me.

We do the same *thang* too, some of the brothers do the same exact *thang*. We start talking about how good the white woman is, or how a foreign woman is, a Polish woman, anything except our own. Then when I start explaining it to them; look around you, look how many different colors and shades we come in—we got black women that look just like they are white. We have black men that look like they're white; some of our presidents probably were black, they look like they are white and their parents were so well to do that they had to keep them inside the house and keep it undercover.

None of this stuff is new under the sun; *ain't* none of this stuff new, the lighter you are, the better your situation will be. A lot of us are black and look white, and we won't even admit that we're black. We refuse to say it, but time will tell. Like I always tell people, we are saving a lot of races--we saved a lot of races. Any race you go to you'll find a black person. So we've been some of everywhere, haven't we? And they can't get rid of us and they keep telling you you're the minority, and in fact, you're the majority. This is why they got to keep miscounting us—that's why they got to keep saying, we're not doing this, and that. This next race of people is the Hispanics, are going to be the minority.

They're having babies so fast—the only reason we're not having them is because we can't afford them. Because it's too hard for us just to make it day-to-day. Here it is you can't even pay your mortgage or your rent on time because of the way your paycheck comes. How many of us can sit down and say till this day, that I got $25,000 dollars sitting up, that I can reach, that I never have to worry about my bills being behind and my job is so secure, that I *ain't* got to worry about losing my job. None of us.

They give things to each other; we can't give each other anything because we have nothing to give. The ones that do, he is so scared of us. We've been taught that we're so bad that it's just engraved in our minds. We can't trust each other. We don't like each other. I'm telling you, the infamous Willie Lynch Letter—"only trust me."

How many times have we seen in our neighborhood, the brother or the sister doing well as far as selling the drugs and stuff? You wonder how come they haven't got busted. Have you ever thought that they're working for somebody in a higher level? That this was meant to be; this was orchestrated? This is to keep you down? This is to keep them there? But then they get so powerful and they want to get out, they can't get out the system. They can't get out. They'll kill them or they'll put them in jail or they'll make some kind of excuse that they did this and all the time they've been working for the government but they've been used. And when they get finished using you, they're done with you. I'm going to lock you up; I'm going to make you disappear. They put you in one of the jails down south.

There are prisons now that they call—for the hard criminals; that will never be able to be reformed. Who said these people can't be reformed? What is it that they have done in order to never be mentally able to be reformed? I can even get set up like this. I have already been put in for mis-identification—misidentified or whatever may have you. It can happen to anybody and it has happened more to us than anybody. Once they get you in the system, they want to keep you in the system. It's called free labor.

If we sit back and look at the way we live, everybody out there, everybody that's reading this book, probably got some kind of dope fiend in the family, somebody that's gay in the family, somebody that's an alcoholic in the family, somebody that's illiterate in the family, and somebody that's making it in the family. How are you scared to come out of your house? How are you scared to get out and mingle in your community and you have the same thing right in the midst of your family?

Somebody on ADC, somebody that's not doing well, you think you're better than them, and they think they're better than you. You cannot get along with. You might even say, "Ooo I can't stand that woman—these people." I'm talking about these people in our family that we feel this about.

Now how come we can't go out here in this real world and that person that's a dope fiend, if he's on dope and he's trying to take something from you or he's doing something to you; you treat him just like you would do that person who is in your family. Man, you might as well get on up out of here with this. You weren't taking it from them.... You would tell him, "Don't come up in here no more; don't do this, go try to get you some help or something." Every time we do that, we tend to get this reaction, "Everybody saying this and that, that's why I'm doing this." You know, I understand.

All I'm trying to tell y'all is how are we scared, and these are supposed to be our kids and our brothers, our sisters, our cousins, our nieces, our nephews. Now how are you scared of your family? We can say what we want to say—that's why they won't let you have your own police community. We used to be able to police ourselves. Soon as they came in policing us, it *ain't* been right since.

This is why you can't have your own jails, we can't have our own, our own, Police Department, we can't have our own bus system, we can't have our own hospitals, we can't have our own garbage collectors--we cannot have these things, if they let you in, you will go through a lot of red tape. There is so much you will have to do to get in there, but what if we had our own? Do you know that's why we have to be integrated? We were making some money that he, the man, couldn't stand it. He had to get some of that money out of us. Where are they getting it from? We got it honestly.

How can the people that taught everybody something, all of a sudden know nothing? Don't get me wrong, I'm not telling you not to love yourself, or nothing like this, or that you are better than this person. All I'm trying to do is tell you to bring yourself up, because they are going to take what I'm saying here and they are going to try to change it around, and say, "You don't like white people? You don't like Spanish people? You don't like...." I didn't say that. This is what they are going to say. All I'm doing is saying what we have accomplished, what we have done, how far we've come, and how much further we can go. This is all I'm saying.

I tell a lot of people, I don't know what my future— my destiny is going to bring me, but I'll tell you one thing, I'm not afraid to die. There are a lot of brothers out here that's not afraid to die. They don't care anymore. When I say they don't care, I mean not as far as death. I'm looking at when I am dead, I do not have to get up any more.

The point I am making here is teach those around you to be leaders. We must do something to get things back in order. Somewhere along the line, we became lost in how to lead. Everyone wants to lead when someone should be followers. There should be a movement in place that will gather our people to learn to work as a team. We must take control of situations and function as a group. None of us are better the one another. We all should have goals set of organizations that will take control of the lives of many to steer everyone in the right direction. When we reach one goal, we will have to reach another. There will be some who will not want to change.

The way it would work is, put people around you who have the skills that you lack to assist you in reaching your goals. Surround yourself with people who are smarter than you are. I understand the things I don't know, it might be somebody out here of my own ethnic background that can help me with it, but this isn't reality. In order to reach our goals sometimes we will have to incorporate other nationalities to assist us. It's called diversity, that's what they're teaching us now. This is becoming a diverse country; we have all types of cultures: people with disabilities, people that are older, people from all over the world.

We are going to have to start trusting somebody, but we must first start trusting ourselves—trusting each other. If I'm doing better than you are, why should it matter? If you're doing worse than me, so what. Why should I be sitting here trying to use this as an excuse to make myself bigger or better than you or you bigger or better than me, or you do something to try to hurt me to bring me down? It doesn't make any sense. It doesn't make any sense. I noticed I've been sitting back watching everyone, they might not like each other but they respect one another.

Keep this in mind even though they respect one another, they will cross each other out. They'll kill their mama for a dollar. When it comes down to them being poor again, or they can't do certain things, they'll take their own family members out. They will hire somebody to kill somebody in their business or whatever have you, so they will not fail.

I'm trying to tell you, why do we have to keep trying to mimic this? Why do we have to try to act like this? We haven't even scratched the surface; it's so deep and I know I can't scratch it all, but all I'm trying to tell us, it's time for us to start coming together.

If we keep putting ourselves above each other and thinking that we're better because we got a lil bit of change, it can be gone in a minute. They can change the color of money, the shape of it -- they're doing it now. So that doesn't mean anything. It's about really being united and doing whatever we have to do to survive. It's coming here now; it's coming in a complete round circle, 360° (degrees) in a circle. We're almost doing a complete circle and everything tend to repeat itself that's why I say, if you don't know your past, you're not ready for the future, because it's easy to be tricked and redone again.

They're rewriting bills and laws, voting and rezoning. We're not looking at the big picture. We're looking at little parts of it. They are looking at the big picture. What would you do if you were a regular street person and you were just thrown into a situation where everyone spoke Standard English and you couldn't use your street slang? How would you react? You would feel out of place and that's worse.

If you put a well-educated person down into the ghetto and they were speaking Standard English and we were using street slang, they would feel out of place. That's the same thing that happened when they put certain teachers in the schools with our children. Some of them were well-to-do, and they couldn't function.

I was looking at it, like all while we were growing up, we were taught that you know, to just get along. But white kids were more or less—I don't know if they feel like we want to kill them all—if they're parents tell them we're going to kill them, but they always see us as criminals, crooks and thugs. We see them as, they are just stealing everything, and they're doing very well. It's almost something like a dog doesn't like a cat; a cat doesn't like a rat, and so on.... But some dogs like cats. You know they always do something to them to make the cat—to make the dog mad or whatever.... So, it's the same way that they deal with it out here. I believe they are afraid if we get any kind of self-empowerment or we become powerful, that we will treat them the way they treated us. I don't know why they see us as violent; we've learned how to be violent once we got over here. We don't do violence until they do violence to us. They automatically have violence; they will kill their parents for money. They'll have their wives assassinated and killed if it had anything to do with *ends*.

We used to have learning cultures, learning centers, and cultures of civilization. We have never been a violent people. If you notice, every time someone do something to us, we forgive them very well, very quickly. We will forgive them very quickly. We tend to forgive and forget, so that goes to show you, our nature is not violent; it's far from violent.

I just wonder and hope that we will be able to teach our kids well. You wonder why your children don't want to go to work or don't want to function. He is sitting there because he has nothing to look forward to. He feels like, every time he goes out into this world, he gets knocked down or pushed back, you even started home wars with yourself.

A lot of the mothers are telling their children that they're no good, just like their no good ass daddy, and you know, just bringing them down. But it ain't the daddy's fault, a lot of times if you look at it, the mother was doing something too. Then she puts the father out, the father couldn't stand on nothing. It is difficult for him to function. He couldn't. Whatever he did, she was never satisfied; she chased him away, and a lot of times, a lot of these ladies out here kickin' it with other people, and the father comes home and catches her doing wrong. Then the mother can call the police to make it seem as if we are the problem, and the police take us away; because it's another form of divide and conquer.

I tell a lot of sisters that they're the mother of creation. All these civilizations have survived because of the black woman. Brothers, if you want a black woman, she comes in all shapes, colors, sizes and styles, we don't have to go out of our race to be doing too much of anything.

I know it's difficult and I know it's hard. The same way with the female, I know it's very difficult and hard to be dealing with us, but we're in this zone. Society beat us down, you beat us down, and then in return, we beat ourselves down, because we feel like we have no out.

When I used to work at Banley's Records, I would sell records for Mr. Banley. I was the delivery man. At that time, I was introduced to the Hebrew Israelites. They studied the Bible a lot. The Hebrew Israelites are vegetarians. I started doing the same thing, studying the Bible and being a vegetarian. During this time, I got a chance to meet a lot of entertainers; show up at a lot of different parties, and eat some of the best foods. This was another part of the culture that you had when they came to America.

When I didn't have anywhere to stay and I was graduating from Malcolm X, I stayed with one of my Spanish friends who is a friend of my sister's, his name was Renee Rivera. We lived over on Augusta Avenue while I was in my last year of college. I had to pay rent in order to stay there, so working at the record shop was helpful. I bought a green, lil' Mustang, to get back and forth to work.

I moved from Renee's house to Bailey's ("Bug") house—Bug's building, and I was paying the rent to keep everything straight, and we had a really good thing going on. This is during the time I met my wife, Marion. Then everything started changing. I got a little serious, and she got serious. Then she became pregnant. It was time for me to go to Alabama because I got recruited to go to Stillman, like I mentioned before, and now till this day, we have two beautiful kids, who are doing really well, and my wife is beautiful.

I used to always pray when I was little, that I could have a house, children and a wife. Now that I have the family…, you know, you pray for the American Dream because you see it *splattered* all up against the TV, all in the papers, and everywhere. But when you get the American Dream, it turns into an American Nightmare. It's a struggle. It ain't like you can just get out here and everything is going to happen for you and everything is going to go smoothly, and all your bills will be paid. Boy, it's not going to work like that.

You're going to always have some ups and downs and some hardships, because if we could be that comfortable, we would. It wouldn't be that much stress on us. You will have time to go back to inventing things. See times done got so fast now, that we don't even invent stuff anymore. A long time ago, we had time to invent. All though we worked hard like we did, we still had slow periods.

If you were lucky, you learned how to play the violin, a harmonica or an instrument. Our forefathers mastered it. Then those that were taught about books—reading and writing, mastered the books, they learned how to read it, and they learned how to do whatever they had to do to survive.

Now we are just doing things, we're just in such a big hurry; we don't even stop to smell the roses. We don't stop to see how blessed we are. What we do is, is stop and do like others; we just complain and complain and complain. What we should do is treat ourselves nice.

When I was about 16 or 17, this old lady came up to me and said, "Young man, when you get married, don't you marry no girl that don't have no mother or father." You know, it makes a lot of sense to me because I found out that a lot of women who don't have a mother or father environment at home, when things get hard, they can't function--they'll get up and run.

Just the other day, I was in a class and questions were being asked, so I asked a question. Afterwards I was pulled to the side by a female, by a bunch of females, they told me, "You are going to have to tone your voice down some, because you scare people with your voice." See that's what the black man's problem has been all along, we always have to adjust ourselves and calm ourselves down but our females they can do whatever they want to do. It's not right. I told one of them just like this, "This is just like when we came over on this boat you said you were going to survive and we better survive too."

This is what they were telling us. Here it is 1996, and they are still telling us we need to calm down. Then when we adjust ourselves, we just start giving up. When you don't adjust yourself, you're considered as a threat, even to your own people. Continue to stay strong and try to be the man that you are. They ain't got to run us all the time.

The way the kids are growing up today—like these brothers that's coming up now—they're trained to lie so well, that they will destroy your life. I have sat here and watched kids do this. They will do it without having any kind of emotions, expressions and no kind of regrets for what they did or how they treat people. They will lie on you and will destroy you. They will stick to that lie till their grave. Since now that they got all these rules about what you can't do to them, these kids are literally rude. I'm not saying anything wrong with the future, but these are our future generations.

We better start teaching children how to be kids, how to have fun. Let them know they don't have to lie. It's just so, so wild and crazy. They will try to ruin your life, so you have to be real careful what you do and say around these kids, because all they're doing is mimicking what they see. Even though you try to teach them right, they will still mess it up.

When they are around their peers or watching TV and you know the environment that they live in, and any kind of change come about can just mess them all up—it just messes them up. When you've been taught the right way of doing things, you cannot accept what others are doing; what is on TV and what is going on in our environment.

If you've been able to do whatever you want to do all of your life, you're not accepting this. You can't accept this. I don't care what you do. You're never going to be able to satisfy everybody. It's always going to be somebody that dislikes you, or say you're doing wrong, even if it's right. They will tell you that it's wrong. They might feel that you are doing a little bit better than they are. You might even give them good advice and they won't accept the advice, you're becoming a threat to them because you are giving them some good advice.

If you don't have the level of education or supposed to be as smart as they are, then to them you are just an everyday laymen speaking in terms they can understand but they will not accept it. Because now it's showing them that they're not as smart as they think they are.

I've seen it before. Every time you move up in your job, it's a lot of white people or someone there that gives you a whole bunch of resistance. You get the glass ceiling effect where it becomes difficult to complete your job, because they feel they are supposed to be so intelligent and we are supposed to be the ones that are dumb and uneducated. Then when you get up there and you take the spotlight--you do your best, you become a threat to them because they think you going to get the next position, and the next and so on and so forth.

It's a complete circle. All of us are going to be placed in the place where we are supposed to be at eventually. Although it seems as if it is difficult to even function and make it out here because the system that is in place is making it very difficult for us; very difficult, but I'm hanging and I hope that a lot of you will hang also.

A lot of us, what I just found out, do not have Wills or Trust. Although, a lot of us don't have anything to Will or an Estate, it's still important that we have the right papers in place if something happens to us. I've just been going through some changes and see how important it is to have a Will.

If you don't know what someone wants when he dies and they can't speak for themselves, you have to make some important decisions, man. So, if at all possible, I know it's probably a wrong place to have this, but start preparing your Will. Looking into what Attorneys are; what kind of rights you have. You'd be surprised how it would make your life a little easier; especially here in America. Just start taking care of personal business—that's one of our problems. A lot of us get jammed because our business is not taken care of when someone we care about dies.

Another thing that should be in place is, you get pulled over by the police, you don't have tags on your car. You get pulled over by the police, you don't even have your driver's license; you don't have a sticker on your window. You didn't take care of your business and now you're going to jail. Now someone can search in your car, now they can treat you anyway they want because you are getting a violation anyway.

We as a black people need to—I'm not saying all of us don't take care of business, but a large majority of us don't take care of business. Then when we do get in some kind of business, we want to go out and buy material things instead of trying to invest the money into something that can make us more money, we buy material things. A lot of us also get tricked because we try to get something for nothing. In America you don't get something for nothing. If it sounds too good to be true, the majority of the time, it is.

You can't double up on this and do all this; it's something illegal about it. All I ask us to do is, slow down; take a real good look at it and analyze it; you ain't got to do everything that's going on right now. If anybody ever pressure you into doing something, most of the time, it's some kind of con game or it's too good to be true.

When you went to school, a lot of us we just sit around on our ass, especially the ones that didn't finish. We had this look on our face of being lost and bewildered, because we don't know what to do with ourselves. A lot of times if you ask most of these brothers how did they get put out of school, they don't even know. They don't even know how they got put out of school.

They don't know if they dropped out or if they got put out. If you don't go to school they just drop you after a certain age, or you get put out or did you just drop out because you wanted to hang out. They really couldn't answer the question. They couldn't tell me if they dropped out or they got put out. Because if at all possible, they need to go back and get some kind of former education because they are not even letting you become a police or work for the fire department, unless you have two years' of education, of college—Junior college. This is the only way you are going to get a salaried job.

Then it will still be hard for you to get in. So all I'm asking is that we start putting more emphasis on education. Everybody can't be a pro baseball player; everybody can't be into some kind of entertainment, dancing and singing. You are going to have to have some kind of talent or skills in order to function until your boat come in—until you able to fit in the mold or whatever have you....

We never know what our destination is going to be, but if we prepare for it, we should be able to be prepared for any situation that comes our way. We should be able to adjust very quickly; we should be able to do it in a timely, comfortable fashion.

I was talking to a gentleman the other day, and he was wondering why I was at ease with myself: because I told him, you have to learn how to conquer yourself before you conquer the world. And when I say that, conquering yourself before you conquer the world, if you go inside yourself and feel inside yourself you know when you are doing wrong, you know when you've done wrong. I know I do, you get these tingly feelings—it's a weird feeling. You know, your hairs stand up and they're also good for defense too.

When you're in a wrong situation or you feel scared or threatened, or you are in a new environment, you don't know what the environment is. It's different to you, so all your senses are working. It's the same way out here. When you are doing wrong, you know what you're doing. I don't care if you're retarded, if your brain is gone, you can· still feel if you're doing wrong. Everybody have that feeling. Unless you know how to just tune it out so bad, you just so hard and so cold that you don't care about these feelings, but they will still be there. It's called a conscious.

You know what you're doing. So, all this about I didn't know what I was doing when I did it, or I did this because I grew up like this, and I couldn't do this because I didn't have this available to me, is piece of crap. I call it the victim card. Put away that victim card and become strong. Just step to the side and just take your time. Again, every time you rush something, you usually make a mistake.

CHAPTER TWELVE

How many of you really just stopped and slowed down and just smelled the different seasons? Do you know how spring smell? Do you know how fall smells; do you know how summer smells? Do you know how winter smell? All these different things are part of our lives and a lot of us haven't taken time to even smell it or to see it; it's beautiful. Just slow down for a minute you got time in between here to see the different seasons, smell them, and sense the way they feel.

This is almost just like our lives, see you got ants, ants ain't got a leader, but you see them, they're just as busy—they're busy all summer long—collecting their food and putting it up so they can have something to eat later. And they all will be able to eat off of it and function.

Squirrels are the same way. You see a squirrel, he is busy burying his food, digging it up, and then when it gets cold, he knows exactly where to go and get it. So, all I'm asking you all is to take some time out for yourselves and smell life. Smell life. It's a beautiful smell. This is a beautiful world. I ain't mad at the world, it's just a lot of the people in it that's messed up.

When you have this attitude, you'll be surprised how comfortable you will be; how at ease you'll be. I don't say my life is just so beautiful that I don't have any problems. It's far from that. I have problems, I have normal problems that everybody else has, but I deal with it in a different way. I take a lot of my anger and put it into something positive. Then when you do it like that, it doesn't bother you either. You are always going to have somebody that's not going to go along with your program. Who is not going to like what you are doing. They feel that you're too happy.

Even on your job, sometimes you'll find out if you are smiling too much, the boss will send somebody to find out why you are so happy. They feel you are supposed to be miserable. Life can become miserable when you look at it negatively. You will have your ups, your downs, your needs, and your wants, your rewards, and your punishments, the truth or the denials. We are going to have all these different things that are going to come about. If we learn to relax ourselves, we are going to be able to deal with any situation, but if we sit around making everything a problem even though it is really not a problem, matters can become worse.

A lot of the times the things that we worry about are really not a problem. Sometimes things are out of our control, then we take a mole hill and turn it into a mountain. We think about it and think about it all the time until it becomes a problem. When we could've sat back for about 20 minutes and take a deep breath and then analyze the situation again and find out that it really wasn't a problem after all.

This is the exact same way with our relationships. When we get mad at each other, we say things we really don't mean instead of saying it at the proper time when we are dealing with the situation, we wait. We wait two, three, or four months later and then when we bring it up, we throw it in their face.

For example, with me and my wife, we try not to go to bed mad. We talk about what is brothering one another. We get it off our chest so that we can deal with it and move on to the next stage because we are only human.

You have the right to say what you want to say, but if you wait three and four months later, this is where the problem starts. That means you're not communicating, you're not able to express yourself around that person or that person is not able to express himself around you. So you're liable to come to a crash down the road somewhere.

Again, I always tell them, a woman is equal, if she is out there working just as hard as you are and she is paying half the bills and you paying half the bills, you should have a good life because you're not carrying all the burdens. Since society got it where everybody has to work, don't put them down, where you still think you're doing this and you're trying to do like the old school where you paint the house, you milk the cows, you fix the car and I do this and that.... No, no, no. It's not like that anymore. Look at that person as an equal, look at them as your partner. Always keep that line of communication wide open, because soon as you shut down that line of communication, that whole system will shut down.

When you all get together, don't fight in front of the kids, don't be going off as far as, when I say something. When I say go left, you go right. Don't fight about money. Try not to anyway. Because of this society's pressure that is placed upon you, you will argue. If you are doing things incorrectly, if you're getting high and all this other stuff, your money ain't goin' to ever be right. A lot of times we have to stop and think about what we are doing and take care of our business.

When we did not have much, I remember we used to always throw the stuff out of the window and my mother would have to go down there and pick it up. We would throw everything out, she was up and down. I also remember when we sat the kitchen on fire one time. We put it out with water. She was gone somewhere and we were trying to cook.

I recall they used to *er*—sit back and be at home and they would eat this starch called Argo starch. They would look at soap operas all day, drink a little Richards, but I think that was the hottest going thing back then.

Back to what I was saying before, we have a lot of sisters that's out here. They have five Children by five different men and not one of them look alike. Then all of a sudden they get mad at you when you can't do anything for them, and then they want to add water to mix and make you turn into an instant dad. Then when they get finished with you, most of them will put you out the house because you ain't got a job. You end up out in the parking lot with the rest of the boys until your other girlfriend or someone wants to pick you up.

If you notice, some of the women are getting a higher education and getting all the jobs while you are out here on the streets trying to do everything you can to survive.

In the predominant minority communities, most are out here selling dope, paying for mama's house. Then get locked up waiting for someone to send you money for commissary, they can't do anything for you, they won't even come visit you. Your baby mama ends up going with your boyfriend, your partner. There's nothing new up under the sun—everything goes around again and again and again.

The way we wear our haircuts now, our parents had their hair cut the same way before, the way they wear their shoes, their pants, all this is the same. Also my Uncle named Billy cut hair and cut it the same way they do now. They would take turns, you cut their hair, and your friends will help you cut your hair, and so on.... You know, you were in the click and everything was cool. Some of you would go out partying together.

The first time I got drunk, I was around about 11 years old, we were in Detroit. My Uncle name David was disabled. He gave me a drink called Ripple. He got me so drunk that we looked ridiculous. A drunk boy with a man in a wheelchair that was drunk, and we got to rolling down the street--the wheels came off the wheelchair--he knew how to put them back on, it was just the outside rubber part that came off the wheelchair, but it was something wild. It was just something real stupid.

The other side of the family used to always make these little model cars. I recall one time we were over at the house because my Mother didn't show up and the family on my Mother's side came and got us. They had these whips and swords, because my Grandfather was an Indian, but they used to have all this kind of stuff lying around. One of the uncles, I can't recall the exact one that did it, but he broke out this bullwhip and he used to pop my brother with it. I was hollering stop and he was popping everybody with this whip, he thought it was fun. This side of the family was always deep—when I say deep, I mean they didn't care for us too tough. We really didn't get a chance to know most of the people on my Mother's side, because they would more or less stay away from us. We did get a chance to meet everybody on my Father's side.

I don't know what the problem was over there, but it seemed like they really didn't want to be associated with us for some strange reason. Now, I let my kids see some of everything. I do not cheat them out of anything. I let them see the hard life, the slow life, the good life, and the rough life. I always tell people like this, you live, you die, you hurt—you cry, you're happy, you're sad, you get sick, or you are on top of the world. You know this is how life goes. Sometimes it's a struggle just to make it, but it's fair, the world is fair if you let it become fair. It all depends on how much you really want to make it out here. Because you are going to have trials and tribulations, as you see—I've been up and down, down and up. Right now, I'm on the upscale, but always leave room for—in case something goes wrong, I can adjust to it.

The entertainment industry is making millions and billions of dollars a year. If they no longer had all this money, what would you think would happen to society? Do you think they would give the entertainers their money? I don't think so. They would tell them to get out their face. Here is a great idea, if all the blacks were to invest their money together and were to do something with it, I'll bet you we would not be able to get our money. They would somehow hold our money up.

A lot of these brothers running around, they don't know if they dropped out of school or got put out of school. Most of us we sit around the house all day looking at TV, or they get up at night, go outside and hang out with everybody at night, and sleep all day. In the daytime, they should be looking for employment because employers are not taking applications after 9:00 at night. This is not the time to go put in an application for a job.

During the holiday times, people get really depressed. A lot of people can't feed their family, a lot of people won't be able to buy anything for their kids for the holidays, but everybody running around saying happy holidays, happy this, happy that. I'm not saying there's anything wrong with the holidays, but if you look into a lot of holidays, you're really spending a lot of money. The holidays wasn't set up for you to spend your money, at least from what we were taught, it was supposed to be a celebration of the life, or the death of something, the creation of something or something. It was supposed to have been something positive, but it has turned negative.

When the holiday season comes around, people start acting rude towards each other. They would hurt one another. This is just part of the environment we are living in now. Holidays are supposed to be family times and happy times, but we done got so material with it, that we just can't even function.

Coming to school was not a fashion statement I wanted to make. It was a time to learn. I wouldn't be raggedy, raggedy, but I would dress plain. I never act like I have money. I don't show that I have money. When I come in, I'm dressed casual with a different attitude. I could wear the expensive $200 shoes, the hats, the works, but if I come in here like this, I'm coming in for a fashion show instead of learning. This wouldn't get me anywhere.

I found out, a lot of the females are able to *peep* you out, they know if you're really poor or if you are just faking, they really know. I don't know how they know, but they know. It's different and I want a lot of the little young brothers to try it. Pull off some of the gold and that jewelry, leave it at home, invest in you an education and see how you turn out.

I also found out that, there are a lot of brothers that I know of who is glutton for punishment. It seems like the more pain and the more pressure we're up under, the better we are at functioning in this society. It makes us better. Although, it seems like the more our females hurt us, the more life hurt us we seem to keep making the same mistakes.

See, I don't like the pain. I can feel it when I hit a pothole. I do not want anything hurting me. If life has to hurt, I'm sorry I am going to try to find something else. If I see you make a mistake, I don't have to do it.

Fellas, I want y'all to start doing something different. I want y'all to try this: 1) the next time you're out with your girlfriend, have an attitude; 2) Er, have your girlfriend pay your gas, light and telephone bill; 3) have her to help you get you an apartment; 4) tell her you want her to co-sign for you a car; 5) tell her you where you want her to go - pick up your partner; 6) tell her you want her to take you and your partner to the barber shop; 7) and tell her you want your cut; 8) tell her you want to go get your nails done. Better yet, when she comes and picks you up, have an attitude and tell her you want her to just drop you off at home. Then she'll say, "What's wrong with you baby?" Do them the same way they treat us, do the-flip the script on them; have an attitude soon as she come over to the house; when she wants to get busy, tell her you're tired see how she handles this. I bet you she won't handle it well, and when she hits you, call the police on her and tell the police she hit you. Tell her you want to press charges. Flip the script on them and see how they like this. I bet you they will not like it at all.

You know what is hilarious to me, some professional women, when they see a brother that's really trying to make it—he's dress-right-dress, they tear him up make him feel like mess.

There are some women who want to come and holla at a brother who got 90 years for murder and rape to get what she wants because there are no ties to him.

I've also found out that most of us once we get married or if we have a girlfriend, find ourselves begging just to be pleased. I feel like this is not right. Ladies, when I say pleased, if you got your real man that don't mind being with you and you are out there doing whatever you want, why do you think you got to hold the sex hostage, this is really the only thing you are giving us, to a certain extent, is a little bit of sex, why are you holding it hostage?

You are going to stay lonely. You are going to be lonely like your mama, mama's mama was. Excuse me for saying your mama mama's, but most of y'all, if you came from that single family environment, you get bored with people, you don't want to—you don't want to stay with one man. You don't want to just be devoted, and it could be vice versa. When you get a man, don't start playing games with him. Be the woman you are supposed to be when you deal with him. Don't play the same games you played when you both got together.

I need to let a lot of the *sisters* know, don't believe your pussy don't stank, it stank. You are sitting up here and you tearing your drawers out; you selling us out; you mixing up with anybody and everybody, then you sit here and you can turn your nose up; then when the material things stop, and your body gets old, you out here all by yourself then you sitting here all confused, and thinking that somebody have done something to you; you out number us.

It's time for y'all to slow down y'all roll and see where you suppose to fit in. I am not telling you to be a slave for no man or something like that, but all I'm trying to tell you is: don't act like you don't know what's happening here—you all getting setup.

YOU are doing what you are supposed to do, and most of y'all turn into dogs like men used to be. You think you can do any and say anything you want to say to people and do anything you want to them. We are supposed to just accept it.

A lot of the brothers are getting tired. We are just tired. We rather just leave you alone. We will leave you alone. If I didn't have kids right now, my name would stop here; I wouldn't even try to give y'all any children. If I didn't have any kids at this time, I would not have any children; it would stop right here.

It's bad that we have to feel this way about our own. If it's any way possible that you all can recover yourselves and come around like you suppose to, we can talk. It would be just fine. I'm not saying all of you, but a large percentage of us have forgotten where we come from and where we are going. It's not that I got anything against females, but all the ones I have ran up on that have any-any type of power, any type of control, she usually takes advantage of it. Wisdom is power, and power is knowledge. Power is used for good, not to abuse others with it. When you abuse power, it will make a whole complete circle and come right back to bite you.

When the male let the female get set up in these positions, please don't abuse your power. The majority of time, if you are a strong black man, they ain't going to let you have too much power anyway. If you are gay or if you humble yourself to a certain extent, adjust to the program, you might go a long way.

Then this is the image that our sons see. If you notice, even when you're a comedian or some of the ball players, they have to dress up like little women to get some attention. The entertainers, you have to act like a little bitch to be able to get some attention.

Here it is, I'm standing here minding my business, and I'm pulled to the side by my own and told that I should tone myself down; tone my voice down, I should do this-uh-uh. This is what the problem with the black man is we keep toning ourselves down and everybody else going ahead while we are still stuck in the same spot.

Look at yourself, how many of us—it's a very small percent – are listed at the Fortune 500, none! When we try to open up businesses, we can't open up any type of business. This is not a mistake because we keep on sitting here humbling ourselves. You are dead already black man. It's time for you to wake up. We're not pointing any fingers. We ain't running around with victim cards, and I'm not trying to get on the Oprah show.

All I'm trying to tell you is, look around and see how many brothers out in the parking lot pushing buggies; collecting cans and don't even know his name, you call his name, hey buddy and he doesn't even know his name; sitting here talking to himself; still getting high; still trying to be slick; still trying to play a game and the games been played on him.

You might not believe this, but every time society recognizes that he's done lost another black man, they have a party. You know they might not be having balloons and hotdogs and music playing, but the more of us that are taken out, this is one strong black male that they have don't have a problem with or dealings with. They bringing in the agents, they bringing in all the foreigners from all over, everybody here is taking care of their business, but the young black male, he's on the endangered species list.

We going to be something like the Indians pretty soon, it will not get that serious because we are the majority all over the world, we are not the minority, we *are* the majority; and we have little young black brothers coming up that's going to be geniuses.

All I'm asking us to do is, is to stand up straight, have good mannerism, so you can carry out great names of your forefathers. Let them recognize your importance; see something that they can relate to, a black man adding to society. Do not bow your head for to anybody because you know, all of them are always smiling at our sisters. They are always winking at our *sisters*, but frown at us. When he comes pass you, he has a hard look on his face. He will tell you, you are a failure. You're far from a failure.

All I'm asking is that you start slowing down, and look at the situation. Every time you look up, it's some white guy in one of our sister's faces, talking about, "Oh Sadie, you look so well today; did anybody tell you how well you looked?" opening the door for her, doing all kinds of things for her, being a true gentleman. We don't have material things to give them and they should know this by now.

I've noticed, the young ladies, they're harder than the young men. They're more boisterous. They're more aggressive. I've noticed that some of the feminine parts of a lot of females have disappeared. I don't know if it comes from single parent's syndrome or what, but the women are more aggressive than the men. They'll choose the man instead of the man choosing them.

It's more acceptable for two ladies to be together than two men. Right now, I'm in class. I noticed that I have more female friends than male. Don't any of them like me, because I got my haircut certain way; they don't like me because I'm black. I understand.

There is nothing but sisters in here and they are all different shapes and colors. (I don't know what y'all is, but y'all don't like black men! I'm going to buy me a couple of pets and some animals and be just like Michael Jackson.)

Okay, now the rumor starts. We have three brothers in the class and six sisters. I don't know where all the brothers are, I think they are out there shooting pool and dice, selling dope and buying somebody's mama a house. I understand, we are going to jail, but I want the sisters to sell dope for me.

Why can't she buy me a Mercedes? Why she can't pay my car note? Why she can't pay my gas, light and telephone bill? My kids need shoes. I need my hair done. I'm telling you, it's time for us to flip the script on these *sisters*, man.

I heard she was kickin' it with somebody else. Soon after I drop her off, she gets in her little ride that I bought her, and go kick it with somebody else with the new fresh hairdo, my new fresh fingernails; I didn't even get to mess up her hair first. Some nigga named Frank-Riding a horse name Roscoe? Roscoe good. Roscoe good, or 357. They got niggas name 357, in jail. Do you understand?

Some of these women, don't want a brother with an education, they go and get a brother straight out of prison knowing that he is not going to last long. Not all of them. I'm not saying all of them.

Thanksgiving is tomorrow and we are celebrating killing the Indians and eating their buffalos. We are going to party. Now you know if they killed the Indians and their buffalos, they are getting ready to kill a nigga next.

We are going to open casinos, and we are walking around here wanting to be like Scarface, Snoop Doggy Dog, and Tupac. I want to make an album called Makaveli, and go out with a girl named Little Kim.

This was a game we played. I remember when we were little we had people that we would call customers; we would go over to their houses and assist them with some odds and ends. When we find a customer, I would tell them it was my birthday, and then I'd come back with one of my sisters and tell them it was her birthday, and I come back with my brother, and say it's his birthday. And then one day, one of the customers says, "How many brothers and sisters do you got?" "And was y'all born a day after each other or what?" We had to quit going to that customer's house.

There was another customer I would go help clean his house. I guess his wife had passed, he had a house full of kids, he just wanted to show them how fortunate they were to have a nice place to live and that they should keep it clean. He brought me over, and I cleaned up the whole house while they were just standing there watching me. He was showing his children how fortunate they were that they had this house, and they wouldn't even take the time to clean it. I thought this guy was more or less of a friend, but when I went back one day to visit them they didn't really want to have too much to do with me.

This is similar to the way me and my siblings are treated on my Mother's side of the family. They really didn't want to have too much to do with us. I've seen even till this day, we would be coming up and we find ourselves explaining what's happening at home, and we always had to explain to some white person.

Just like over in Luanda in South Africa right now, they just showed us this white lady from New York or somewhere, she's taking in all these black people and making them do the religious dance, but they all got on blonde hair. She is supposed to be saving them but she really wasn't. The same way they did during the time of the Underground Railroad. They let a few of us get by, but kept most of us.

Again, this is why I keep telling you, history constantly repeats itself. The Willie Lynch Letter says not to trust each other, only trust them; they are the only ones that can save you. It's like that now even when the police pulls you over; if it's a white one and it's a black one, the black one don't always be the one that treats you kind of hard and rough, and the white one says, "All you have to do is be cool, you need to wait a minute." They play the give and take, but this is what we have been trained to do.

We should start taking notes of the things that we do. The times constantly repeats itself. If we do not keep track, it will take advantage of us. We will become extinct. One day we will wake up and they will say, all black people or all foreigners or all whoever, report to your slave station?

The only reason I'm putting all of these different things in my book is because they won't say that I'm just anti-white or anti-black and I'm this and that. I do not have any hatred towards any group or nationalities. It is more of a conspiracy towards the black male if anything. If I don't have any homosexual tendencies towards myself, I can't function or be able to get into the program. I'm sitting here right now watching them. It's more of them with a little sugar in their tank or pretending to have it in their tank than anything.

The strong black male is not down in the administrative office, they are not in the higher level office, and then when you do get there, after they get finished using you, they will tear you down.

As far as the drug dealers, politicians, when we worked in the south, and we brought the south back, after they got finished, we could not be governors or things of this nature. They took us down. And then we had one black governor, as he became governor, he went to jail for some kind of high or somebody was doing something illegal.

All I'm trying to say is that, once we get in a position, if we're not weak, you would not stay on that job long; black males. Again, this is not an excuse, this is not saying the world is treating all black males bad or anything like that, but again, if you're strong, you have problems with your wife, you be strong, you have problems with life, you be strong, you have problems on your job, if you're strong, you have problems period.

We do not want to see strong black males. They will hinder you in any way possible. We would rather see you in a penal institution, than a higher learning. Again just now, I just spoke to a white teacher that just came in through here. I said, "hello, how you doing?" He looked at me like he hated me or something. And it's a black African lady behind the desk, she says, "Hello Ray," he damn-near jumped over the table to see her. I wasn't speaking a foreign language. I was speaking Standard English.

It's another brother that's sitting to my left and my right, and this man will speak to the gay one, watch. Yes he did. On the other hand, the other brother looks really strong. He hasn't said anything to him, won't even make eye contact with him; and it's *kinda* weird.

They will not even make eye contact with you; and I am not sure. It's time for this madness to stop. And when I say African, I'm talking about the ones that are over here from the continent of Africa; she's from there. She's from the islands. But she's European, European oriented, more-she does not even recognize us and it's weird. She looks me dead in the face and just looked like I have done something to her.

Now when he came in there he was smiling and everything. We *try* so long and so hard, not to trust each other and to lie on each other, that it just comes automatically.

I hope this book doesn't offend anybody or make anybody mad. I would hope that this book will be more of an eye opener of life and things that life has in store for you if you do things in good faith and honesty, you will have great success.

First you have to figure out how to structure your destiny, which direction your destiny is going in and what to do when these goals are reached? Once you reach them and they're met, what to do with it?

Secondly, do not feel guilty about those who will be left behind. There is always going to be some that you can't please and some that you will please.

A lot of the stuff that I'm sharing in this book is common sense and everyday life, that we must deal with and we will deal with which comes with its own set of problems. We will have all types of different problems that we are going to have to solve. There is nothing you can do about this, but adjust to it, because a lot of these things are out of our control and we try to make something out of it that it's really not. All I know is, is that a lot of us do a whole bunch of rushing, a whole bunch of rushing. We don't take time to smell the coffee, feel the bumps in the road, etc....

BIO

Melvin Dukes was born in Cleveland Ohio. He moved from city to city. Mr. Dukes served in the United States Army. He is a veteran.

Dukes attended college and earned a Ph.D. in business administration. He is a Divine 9 Kappa Alpha Psi Fraternity, Inc. and a Master Mason.